THINGS

NO ONE

TAUGHT US

ABOUT LOVE

T0347185

THINGS

HOW TO BUILD

NO ONE

HEALTHY RELATIONSHIPS

TAUGHT US

WITH YOURSELF AND OTHERS

ABOUT LOVE

VEX KING

bluebird
books for life

Some of the material from this book was
previously published as Closer to Love, 2023

First published 2024 by Bluebird
an imprint of Pan Macmillan
The Smithson, 6 Briset Street, London EC1M 5NR
EU representative: Macmillan Publishers Ireland Ltd, 1st Floor,
The Liffey Trust Centre, 117–126 Sheriff Street Upper,
Dublin 1, D01 YC43
Associated companies throughout the world
www.panmacmillan.com

ISBN   978-1-0350-4441-2

11

A CIP catalogue record for this book is available from the British Library.

Typeset by Palimpsest Book Production Ltd, Falkirk, Stirlingshire
Printed and bound by CPI Group (UK) Ltd, Croydon, CR0 4YY

Visit **www.panmacmillan.com/bluebird** to read more about all our books
and to buy them. You will also find features, author interviews and
news of any author events, and you can sign up for e-newsletters
so that you're always first to hear about our new releases.

You are worthy of love that is pure, inspiring and wholesome: the kind of love that unlocks your capacity to love yourself more deeply, especially in those testing moments when your mind vigorously swims against the tides of pain. You deserve to be loved by someone who exercises patience and understanding, offering a compassionate ear. Someone who invites you to be vulnerable with their warmth and holds tightly to the revelations of your heart. May they cherish you entirely, embracing all parts of you, including the ones you've been struggling to accept.

But first, you must return to where love lives –
in the sanctuary of your own heart.

Contents

Part Two: First Connections

Part Three: Cultivating Healthy Bonds

Part Four: The Realities of Relationships

Part Five: Letting Go With Grace

Share images or videos of your favourite pages, quotes and experiences related to this book on social media using #VexKing so I can see them and share them across my platforms.

For more inspiration, follow my social media platforms (all @vexking).

Preface

I wrote this book to empower you to enrich your connections with others.

Consider this the concentrated extract of years spent delving into the mysteries of the heart. You'll find no filler here – only concise truths crafted to awaken your highest potential for deep and fulfilling relationships.

While I've curated this paperback book into bite-sized portions, my previous hardback edition, *Closer to Love*, offers a more extensive read should you wish to dive deeper.

In this book, I feature a few real-life and some made-up examples of relationships. But I want to be clear that these scenarios apply to all genders and different couplings. Love is love, as we're about to learn.

May the pages ahead quench your thirst for self-knowledge as we explore the journey of love and relationships together.

Introduction

For most of my childhood, life was a struggle. My single mother had to work exceptionally hard – not only to secure a home that we could call ours, but to put food on the table in that home. She worked tirelessly to make money and survive, and to take care of us, her three kids.

My mum would save up where she could, and our weekly tradition was renting a Bollywood movie from a local sari shop that had a hidden shelf stacked high with VHS tapes. The films we rented were all musicals telling romantic love stories. Actors and actresses sang their hearts out to each other in random places, with the quirkiest dance moves and deepest displays of affection (always PG, of course).

My earliest lessons on romance instructed me that love meant: 1) exaggerated gestures of desire, and 2) the protagonist's unrelenting need to end up with his beloved . . . whom he had met only days before.

These movies were teaching me that life is one big love story – it's the journey to find the person of your dreams. And that once you find them, everything will be OK – as long as you can both dance.

In reality, it doesn't quite work like that. Don't get me wrong, life *is* one big love story. We express love for many people and things during our time here on Earth. It's our biggest motivator. And a relationship is a dance of sorts.

But the films only ever showcased the highlight reel of relationships. Delete and edit out all the work, hardship, misunderstandings – and *bam*, there's your happily ever after. Roll credits.

And they neglected the most important thing: the inner journey we all have to go on to be triumphant in love. The journey where we defeat our insecurities, reckon with shortcomings, battle our demons and find a deep appreciation and love for ourselves.

When we skip or fast-forward this personal work, the unresolved emotional issues inside of us get projected onto relationships. Without doing the internal work first, connections become breeding grounds for drama and suffering. Internal conflicts must manifest somehow; if it isn't through self-work, it will be at the expense of those we love most.

· · ·

Growing up, we look for templates of what relationships look like. Generally, our caregivers will – for better or worse – provide us with our earliest examples. We also have the idealized templates we're exposed to through popular culture – whether that's Bollywood or Hollywood, art or books, the media or music. It's these fairy tales that, more often than not, take a hold in our imagination and provide the templates we aspire to for our own love stories.

Take Millennials, like me, and more recent generations, like Gen Z. We have grown up in an era where social media dominates – and it plays a massive part in how we approach relationships. We've become accustomed to labelling cute selfies or staged images as 'relationship goals' – goals we establish through single snapshots.

So, we collect all these expectations of what love and relationships should or should not be. We crave, demand, yearn for love – our happily ever after. Because we believe that when we find 'the one', all of our problems in life will be solved. When we don't find perfection or have all of our needs met, or when we encounter disappointment, we struggle. We think something is wrong with the other person, or with us, or the whole idea of love itself.

We believe that we need a better half because we are not whole.

We look for someone to complete us because we've decided we're incomplete.

We carry our insecurities, conditioning, trauma, unmet needs and pain into relationships, only to be met with instances that create more of it.

And on top of all of this, a thick defensive wall has been put up around our collective world-heart, and love struggles to find a way in.

So many of us are lost when it comes to relationships, connections, familial ties and friendships. If you were to read through my Instagram DMs, you would see this as clearly as I do. Much of what I hear has to do with people trying to make their relationships work. Because we want them to work. Ghosting people, speed dating and relationship-hopping don't serve your spirit and can make the yearning for love even greater.

The most common questions, concerns and sentiments I hear include:

- 'My relationship would be wonderful if my partner would just do x/y/z.'

- 'I'm tired of having my heart broken. How can I keep it from happening?'

- 'The ghosts from my past are haunting my new connections.'

- 'If I can change, why won't they?'

Others who are already on a healing journey want to know:

- 'How can I love unconditionally while maintaining healthy boundaries?'

- 'I feel like my relationship lacks depth; how can I take it to the next level?'

- 'I want to understand them better, but it feels impossible.'

- 'Why do I continuously attract people who betray or abandon me?'

A lot of people feel like failures when their relationship breaks down, blaming themselves for not doing enough or not 'being' enough.

When love and connection are what we most desire, why is it so hard to get it right?

• • •

Here's what I want you to hold on to. Love is a human need – a birthright. We all deserve it. It's essential to our development and quality of life. But we have to understand that love is an internal experience. It is found and felt from within. A relationship can help you cultivate more love, but ultimately – like a mirror – it will only amplify the abundance or lack of love you carry towards yourself.

While no relationship is perfect – and neither are any of us – I believe that those who genuinely love themselves, who value their own time and energy, can recognize people who love and operate from the same level of awareness. By learning to tend to your own emotional needs, you won't be looking to outsource them to another. This makes it easier to find someone who's compatible with you. It lets you simply enjoy another person as they are, loving them with all of your heart – purely and deeply.

When we fulfil most of our own needs for ourselves, it creates space for relationships to become something greater. Instead of partnerships built on obligation, dependency or bargains, we can experience connections that transcend the transactional. By nurturing ourselves first, our relationships become free to reach new heights, no longer weighed down by expectations or voids seeking to be filled. Independence and wholeness attract something far more profound than co-dependence.

Love and relationships are not quite as we see them in the movies. They're not about finding the perfect home; they're about coming home to yourself, then choosing someone who aligns with you – and with whom you can share your life.

How we misunderstand love

Many misunderstandings accumulate around love. It gets equated with being head over heels, with sappy romance, or even with owning and controlling another person.

One of the most common misconceptions springs from using the words 'love' and 'relationships' interchangeably, like synonyms.

In our journey together we're going to challenge that idea, as well as debunk many other myths and misunderstandings surrounding love and relationships, and try to get at the heart of the truth.

Because at its core love isn't complex. It's a direct experience. It can get clouded by clever words and ideas, but the knowledge of love comes from living it. We feel love throughout our entire being – in our bodies, hearts, minds and spirits.

As a concept, love is jaded, but as a direct experience, it is always fresh.

I'm a strong believer in the power of love and its ability to help us lead full, blissful lives when we are given the right tools to do so. I hope to equip you with the insight you need to experience the love that we all deserve.

As you read the pages that follow, I would like to invite you to go beyond the words. Allow yourself to hear the echoes of wisdom in your own core, and to feel the sense of truth in your own heart.

Let's take the first step by going directly to the source of it all. We are going to investigate the true nature of love.

The right partner
will not complete you.
You are already whole.

The right partner will
expand you. They will
catalyze your growth
and elevate your
consciousness.

PART ONE

The Nature of Love

There is only one love

The love you are searching for is within you. It is you.

At first glance, love seems like a walk in the park. Stop to look a little longer, though, and you'll see it's not just a walk – it's a mysterious wild hike through a jungle of emotions, a quest that has fuelled epic tales since forever.

The pursuit of love is the original blockbuster that never gets boring. And it's a major plotline in just about everyone's own life story.

So, how is it possible that, as a species, *we can't seem to explain what we most long for?*

Love is not scientific. It's not mathematical. It's not exactly rational. And yet it's so simple that even a baby knows what it is, at least on some primal level.

How do we make sense of this apparent contradiction?

Think of it this way: the ocean tastes the same whether you are in Hawaii, Cuba or Australia. Love has the same basic texture, the same basic flavour, no matter the outward expression. Outwardly it is many and varied, but inwardly it is one.

As human beings, we try to fit wondrous experiences into conceptual boxes. But love cannot be boiled down to a formula. Love is the easiest thing we'll ever do, be, experience, give and receive.

It's all the things blocking love that are complex and demand navigating.

Love wears different costumes in various relationships. The way you love your partner is like a Broadway production, distinct from the profound, protective love you feel for a child or the buddy-buddy camaraderie with your best friend. But the love itself is the same. There is only one love, yet this love carries a million colours – and you are a living source of them all. If we're lucky, we get a glimpse of all of them throughout our lifetime.

We can love our favourite places, or interesting things – like keepsakes, books or old cars. We can love our jobs or careers. We can love our bodies, or the body of another human being. There's always room in the heart to love one more thing. If we are wise, we can even love ourselves.

All of these outward forms of love are linked to people or objects. We equate the love we feel with the person, or the thing, that we love. When we 'have' the object, the love is there. When we lose it, love goes with it, leaving a painful void. We feel the absence of love as an ache in our heart.

Love is at the centre of our being

The 'one love' mentioned above starts to tie things together. Some people call it unconditional love. You might also call it big love, universal love, or, if you prefer, divine love.

Despite its fancy and somewhat woo-woo-sounding aliases, it is the one most real thing. It has no separation, and it is not linked to any object.

This is the OG love spoken about by the great teachers of humanity, and the kind of love we encounter during mystical or peak experiences, or sometimes during altered states of consciousness. We feel it in nature or in the ocean. If we are sensitive, we can see it behind the eyes of every creature we meet.

Love may have an infinite number of outward expressions, but it has one basic common feeling. There's an analogy I find useful to help understand love in this way.

Imagine love as a ball. At the centre of the ball is one pure love, unchanging and always there. This love takes on different forms on the outside of the ball – the love between family, friends and even couples. The everyday world we experience is like the outside (the circumference) of the ball, it is forever on the move. The centre, at the core, is our source of life and love, always constant, and it's as if one love is exploring an infinite number of ways to express itself anew. That centre is our source of life, and our source of love. It has no shape or form, but it has one taste, like the ocean. We all recognize it. We can't find it outside of us, but we can find it within.

At its core, the one true love is unconditional and boundless. It recognizes our intrinsic connection to all living beings and to life itself.

This love is not confined to physical proximity or personal relationships, it extends to the whole of existence. It understands that we are in a relationship with everything around us. We are like ripples in a river, connected to the water that flows through us and around us. Although we may seem separate, we are one with the water.

Our personal, more limited, love is felt in our own centre, in our hearts. When we feel this love, we connect with the centre of all things for a moment, and we feel happy and satisfied. The heart of us is connected to the heart of everything. We realize we are not alone; we are all connected.

You are the love you crave

The trouble is that life plays out on the outside of that big ball. On the surface of things, everything changes, and very soon we find that we've lost our connection to love. We imagine that our love depends on a person or the object of our love. When it disappears, as all things eventually must, we think the love has disappeared too.

All our lives we are searching, searching for love, and we're looking for it in the wrong place. We are searching in the world of forms, on the circumference of life, which never stays the same. It keeps slipping away. We look for it from our parents. We try to find it from our siblings or furry friends, and all the other places we have mentioned already. We hold out for that one special love. 'When I find that one,' we think to ourselves, 'I will be happy and whole.'

We may find temporary, or even lifetime, reflections of love on the surface of things, but we can't find the source there. Little do we suspect that we are carrying it with us in our very own centres.

We have to turn the search inwards to find it.

All our lives we are trying to attract love from the outside, when all along we could be shining it out from within. Many of us simply don't know how to do that. Nobody taught us how to shine love.

There is no need to search for what isn't missing. Love is not an Amazon package that goes MIA. We only need to return home to our hearts.

You *are* that love, it is your nature, deep in your centre. Your journey through life, your relationship with another human being, is a reflection of that.

The rest of this book explores how to bring the surface and the centre of the ball – our personal relationships and boundless universal love – together in harmony.

You *are* love, it is your nature, deep in your centre.

Your journey through life, your relationship with another human being, is a reflection of that.

Love is being, relationships are doing

Love is not all you need to be with someone. You can love anyone, but that doesn't mean you should be in a relationship with them. Compatibility, respect, trust, reciprocity, vulnerability, intimacy, communication, understanding and honesty are needed.
Effort is a must.

One reason why we're confused about matters of the heart is our tendency to use 'love' and 'relationship' interchangeably, as if they were one and the same.

For instance, we think to ourselves: 'I love this person, so obviously we must be together in a relationship, even if it hurts.' Or we think to ourselves: 'I'm not in a relationship, so my life is empty of love.'

Love exists independently of relationships. Yes, they're linked, but the two are different things.

Love is an internal state of *being*. It shines from within us, regardless of what's happening around us. It is something that arises out of us, and something that flows through us, like a flavour or a fragrance that's part of who we are. Love is open to receive and it is willing to give. It's a warm, accepting, welcoming flow from our essence.

Relationships are an external state of *doing*. They are about translating love into actions. In a healthy relationship, the state of being in love should, ideally, motivate and guide the state of doing, leading to actions that strengthen the bond and connection between partners.

The love that we 'are' comes alive and takes form in the relationship that we 'do'. We can sit, doing nothing, and still be in love, but if we want a rewarding relationship, we will have to get up off the couch.

Our love has its permanent home in the centre of our being, whereas relationships play out on the surface, changing and moving.

We can't create love – it already exists within – we can only open the inner gates or close them. However, we *can* create, build, sustain and nurture relationships, and work at those.

Relationships need at least two people. Love is an internal experience. So, the essence of love does not require a relationship. We can feel love for anyone, but that doesn't mean we should be in a relationship with them. We can love someone who is no longer with us or who is separated from us by distance. Our real love doesn't depend on body chemistry or bank balance – these are only important on the surface of life; true love reaches into our core.

When a love bond is so deep that it connects two people from the centre of their being, the link is secure. When the link exists only on the surface of things, it remains unstable.

Cultivating love together

Basing relationships solely on passionate emotions sets us up for disappointment, since those feelings fluctuate. Passion burns hot, then fizzles like an Alka-Seltzer in water. But true love? That can simmer on the back burner forever.

Don't get me wrong, the chemistry that stems from romance is still magical, exciting and one of the best feelings in the world. Who doesn't like belting out love songs in the shower while thinking about someone they feel deeply for? But a spark without fuel cannot sustain a flame.

Love is the spine that holds the book together,
but it isn't the full story.

Lasting relationships, romantic or otherwise, require layers of compatibility, attraction, understanding and hard work. If you're entering a relationship to make yourself feel good, you're going about it backwards. You should be there to care for the health of the relationship – to maintain a robust, safe and supportive space for both people. Love may always be present, but relationships need continuous effort to sustain the connection.

Love is the state of being that you experience with someone, and a relationship is the commitment you make to that person – to continue to cultivate love together. As a result, you may experience emotions such as bliss, ecstasy or fiery passion, but those will likely fade. You may also feel calmness, belonging or tranquillity. These sensations may not be as exciting, but they will last longer.

A relationship is like a garden that two people decide to nurture because they really want to. Both people dedicate their time, effort and attention to it, and as the garden thrives, so the experience of love grows.

A cultivated garden needs to be tended regularly in order for the plants to flourish. When they do, we do . . . and we experience the beauty of love around us.

Love is the internal experience that naturally occurs when two people commit to taking care of each other, as well as their relationship garden. If we choose to move on, it doesn't mean we never experienced love, or that we will never feel love for that person again, it just means we no longer share the same garden – the one that helped us generate love. That garden exists outside of us, as a shared space, but the source of love has another home.

Love always happens within

Love is always experienced within. Falling in love with another person is about being in the presence of someone who has led us to recognize our own ability to access love.

When we're loved, it's as if the other person has reached down into their inner river of love, scooped up some water and shared it with us. It feels good. Nourishing. We recognize the wholeness of that love when we realize it has come from the same river of love that exists within us. Water flows into water, and love joins with love.

There is a meeting and a recognition. Their love-driven actions help us recognize our own love within. We experience love as a state of being, because of the love they extended.

When you feel love because of what you receive or experience, from where does the feeling of love arise? The experience is not coming from an external body, from a winning scratch card, a large payslip, a diamond ring or a beautiful car. The state of love that you are experiencing is happening within you. It spontaneously appears somewhere in the heart of you, and that's where you feel it.

Beautiful life experiences are an invitation to dance in the love that you're made of, but the music you dance to always plays within. Wherever you are, love is ready to express itself like sunlight bursting through clouds – sometimes as a quiet glow filling the sky, other times as dazzling rays that take your breath away. But it's always there, shining from your core, ready to illuminate each moment with meaning.

People, actions and external things evoke and awaken the love that's already present within us. To feel the love of another, we must first have discovered it within ourselves. Other people's actions and behaviours can simply make that discovery easier or harder for us.

Love nourishes us

Picture this. Inside each of us, at the centre of our being, is a huge tank of love. It's like having a fancy water source in your back garden. Unfortunately, many of us haven't figured out how to tap into it or use it wisely. But that's the 'secret method' we're going to explore later – self-love.

This love tank is like the fuel for your spiritual engine, the VIP pass to function and think clearly. It's your personal energy drink, without the excess caffeine and sugars. It quenches your thirst and turns you into the superhero version of yourself, ready to share that pure love water with others.

Other people who are struggling to tap into their own tank of love might eye up yours. They're dying of thirst, and your love oasis looks like the solution.

So, they might come along and propose some type of relationship deal to get unlimited access to your tank. They might say, 'Hey, we should be in a relationship together. Here's what I can offer in exchange for your love water.'

They then hand you a cup of fluid. It looks like water, but it's actually something else, like coffee, a soft drink, or even alcohol. As you're already familiar with the taste of pure love water, and you're not thirsty enough to settle for anything else, their offer won't interest you. It's not a fair exchange. It would be like trading a nugget of gold for a pebble. You might hand them a cup so they remain nourished, but a long-term deal for a relationship is off the cards.

You realize it's better to wait for someone who's sipping from their own tank of love. Someone who's not just handing you a drink but guiding you back to your own love oasis. Together, you create an awesome stream of pure and refreshing love. You build a love empire, one sip at a time.

To know the real nature of love, we first have to know our own real nature.

Find someone who will
help you return to the love
within yourself, over
and over.

The real you is radiant love

'As you dissolve into love, your ego fades.
You're not thinking about loving, you're just
being love, radiating like the sun.'
Ram Dass

I'm a lover of the sun. That fiery ball in the sky is like a glowing picture of our essential nature.

The sun shines upon everything on Earth, helping life to grow and thrive. Sunlight not only makes plants grow so that we have food to eat, it also allows us to see and enjoy all the beauty around us. When the sun shines on a landscape, for instance, or on the face of our loved one, the light allows us to fully appreciate those blessings in our lives. Even our selfies and photos come out better in natural sunlight!

The sun shines on everything without judgement – both the good and the bad, the pretty and the ugly. Its light may reveal the kindness in a person's face, or the beauty of holy places; but the sun also shines on rubbish in the streets. The light isn't changed by the things upon which it shines. Shining on palaces doesn't make the sun royalty, and shining on rubbish doesn't make the sun less bright. The sun just illuminates whatever is there without deciding if it's good or bad.

The infinite nature of love is like the sun: it sees all things and all people as inherently worthy of its light. It shines on the good and the bad equally. That same radiating love is your essential being. You are sun-like in your core, radiating life energy that allows you to grow, heal and thrive.

You radiate consciousness, which allows you to see and experience life through all your senses. The gift of life is for all beings 'good', 'bad', 'pretty' or 'ugly'. The light of your consciousness shines on the good and the bad alike.

We don't usually think of ourselves in this way. We certainly don't think of our role in relationships in this way.

Where there is light, there are also shadows. We can so easily focus only on our shadowy troubles in life, forgetting all about the radiance.

This shadowy side of life, love and relationships – namely, the challenges, the troubles, the fear of loss, the fights and the ugliness – all these things happen because of obstacles in the light.

Shadows form when something blocks out the light. The edges of the obstruction create the edges of the shadow. It's the same with our inner barriers to love. The biggest barrier to love is what might be called our ego.

The shadow of the ego

It was Sigmund Freud who made that word 'ego' world famous – at least in the way we use it today. ('*Ego*' is the Latin word for 'I'.) For Freud, the ego was the function of our rational mind that makes decisions. In his theory of psychology, the ego was like a nervous middle-man, constantly negotiating between our powerful animal instincts and our idealistic higher morals.

In this book, the word 'ego' has a slightly different, slightly deeper meaning. Here, when we use the word 'ego' we mean the part of us that is not permanent. It's not the permanent source of light at our core that is continuously shining love, which we just described; instead, it is what we paint on top of that, like a mask.

In this book the ego is 'the story of me' that we spin in our heads, covering our natural core. In this mental story, which we constantly and compulsively create, we may cast ourselves as the hero, or we may be the victim. The point is – it's not a real thing, it is only fiction.

Ego is the part of us that is learned and conditioned. It is the part of us that was told what to do by our parents. It is the educated part of us, and it is who we imagine we're supposed to be in the story. It's what we fear, and what makes us tense, and it's the thing that makes us feel unworthy.

Like a game of Telephone, the ego often retells things incorrectly. The voice in your head that formed early on in life is riddled with coping mechanisms you needed as a child. As a kid, you may have needed to build walls to stay safe. But what protected you then weakens you now. As you build a garden in your adult life, the tools must change; a hammer can't do what a shovel must.

When young, your inner voice used defence tools such as denial, blame or control. Imagining worst-case scenarios may have served as preparation for potential pain. As an adult, though, those tools don't help you grow. Now you're building a garden that needs care and nurture. Hammers, once useful, now risk crushing delicate shoots.

The ego is often what our parents, our teachers and other people want us to be, or what we imagine they want us to be, but not what we naturally are, deep down.

Let's explore this just a little bit more. What is our ego shadow?

Ever notice how you turn into a totally different person depending on who you're with? Got a job interview? Suddenly you're wearing a fancy professional mask, using big words like 'synergy' and ensuring you enunciate every word correctly. Date night comes around? Break out the witty banter and the boring holeless socks. And when your parents are nearby? Be on your best behaviour.

We're all out here playing dress up, trying on identities depending on who we're with. When we're young, we meticulously copy the cool kids' styles, the way they talk, who they crush on. We'd do anything to fit in and figure out who we are.

As we go through life, each new person, each new circumstance, reveals a new aspect of who we think we are. We are one person to our parents, another to our children. We may act like a different person around our colleagues or friends, and this is always in flux. Over time, our personalities, interests, tendencies, hopes, dreams and desires change too. The hero in the 'story of me' goes through transformations.

Who is that person, really?

On top of this, some people might try to label us or belittle us by telling us who and what we are. If we believe those labels, we will start acting a lot like the person they think we are. We become the limited person they see. This can make it impossible to build authentic connections. How can we desire to be loved for who we are when we haven't figured it out yet?

Along the way, who we really are – that radiant love – is obscured by inner barriers, and we cast different shadows as we change over time.

I want to show you that love's light always shines, though your obstructions may make it seem like darkness.

If we can remember that the centre of our being is pure, radiating love and awareness, we can begin to reduce the shadow of the ego. Living from this space, the ego becomes a kaleidoscope of colours instead of casting shadows.

Real love rises above the ego

'Your task is not to seek for love, but merely to seek and find all the barriers within yourself that you have built against it.'
Rumi

Let's keep exploring this idea of the ego and the shadow it casts over our true selves. I want to give you an example of how this could look in real life.

Imagine a boy named Dwayne. Since he was a child, Dwayne has cultivated a strong ego identity around being an 'intellectual' person. He prides himself on being smart, reads complex books and uses big words when speaking. He looks down on those he sees as less intelligent. When he's right, and when he can show it, his sense of self gets a boost, and he feels big and strong.

There's a catch, though. When someone makes a comment that contradicts his worldview, Dwayne becomes defensive and has to prove them wrong. It has become a compulsion. He has heated arguments trying to display his intelligence. When he hears about a friend's success, he feels jealous rather than happy for them. After all, Dwayne believes his intelligence is more worthy of success than theirs. If they are big, that means he must be small, and that doesn't work for him. He resorts to being a critic.

Dwayne is completely identified with the ego story in that he is an intelligent expert. His sense of self *depends* on being the smartest person in the room. He acts from this ego identity constantly, rather than from his true essence. He is led by ego rather than awareness. Dwayne has forgotten the essential human being that he was as a child. He is totally absorbed in the wonderful, painful story of Dwayne's mind.

This causes Dwayne stress as his ego is threatened so easily. If someone feels like a threat to his identity, he will do his best to protect it – sometimes by attacking the other person. If someone makes him feel unintelligent, whether intentionally or not, he might feel like he's not smart enough.

Dwayne is unable to hear the perspectives of other people. As he listens, he's not really there. Instead, he's already thinking about how to argue in response. He cannot accept mistakes or appreciate those with different talents and views. This is his number one problem in all his relationships.

By believing his ego's narrative, he suffers, and he causes others to suffer. Releasing the grip of his 'intellectual' identity would allow Dwayne to access deeper understanding and connection. He is afraid to do that – because who would Dwayne be then?

Spoiler alert, he'd be pure love. When the curtains of the ego fall, the purest and yet most vulnerable parts of us are exposed. Why are we so afraid to see that we are the love we need?

Awakening to love

All of us have the compulsion to play these ego games in life. Our story may not be like Dwayne's, but it is there nonetheless. We imagine we're supposed to be someone, and we try very hard to be someone special. We forget that we are merely playing roles, and we forget all about our true, natural essence. Our real essence is childlike, and accepting, and it has a sense of awe and simplicity, full of compassion and wisdom.

Here's the thing. If we can rise above the image that our mind has created about ourselves through stories and judgements, we can uncover our true nature – a Self of unconditional love, just like the sun.

Knowing this truth means that we can't be affected by the image of who we are that someone else is attempting to create. We begin to know that what others think of us is not who we truly are. This is the deepest level of Self-love (with a capital 'S'), because it's a recognition of our wholeness, as we'll see in the coming chapters.

This truer Self is like the light of love, and like the light of consciousness itself. It reveals our mind's activity, observing all our thoughts and feelings with grace.

We can keep identifying with our ego – and the shadows it casts – or we can let love shine through so that we clearly see where ego causes obstacles. As long as we believe we are only our ego-self, we blame outside things for blocking our loving light. But this love is always there, shining within. We must not forget our loving essence just because others fail to see their own light reflected in us.

When we live on 'autopilot' and don't pay attention, the ego maintains control by keeping us caught in habitual ways of thinking, conditioned from the past. By interrupting, or blocking, our pure presence, the ego tricks us into identifying with old conditioning that helps solidify its false identity.

It's like you're sleepwalking through life. Alarm goes off, feet hit the floor, you rush through the morning routine then zone out during the commute. Next thing you know, you've gone through a whole day on autopilot, absorbed in your thoughts and habits but not really present.

The ego acts like it's all of who we are; but the ego is just a creation of our mind. We can rise above our ego stories, and the benefits can heal and inspire our relationships. We'll expand on this later. For now, let's look at another misunderstanding involving the idea of attachment.

Authentic love gives, attachment needs

Non-attachment means caring without trying to control – and without being controlled by – people, circumstances and outcomes.

Spiritual teachings and psychology view attachment quite differently.

In spirituality, 'attachment' means clinging to impermanent things and people. This is the root of suffering, because the more we try to control an outcome, the more we set ourselves up for disappointment when reality doesn't meet our expectations.

There is great truth in that view. It is precisely because we desire things to turn out a certain way that we fight, stress and obsess. It is because we fear that they might not turn out that way that we suffer. This clinging to 'me' and 'mine', and the story we are so invested in, or attached to, is exactly what makes us tense and anxious. It is the root of our deepest fears, including the fear of loss. Accepting things as they are brings great peace to us, freeing up wellsprings of energy in us to actually change the things we are able to change.

In contrast, psychology regards 'attachment' as a completely normal emotional need for closeness. Attachment theory was introduced by psychologist John Bowlby, then expanded upon by Mary Ainsworth in the 1970s, and it explains that the safety and security of our early relationships with caregivers influences the types of relationships we form throughout life.

Those with secure attachments as children are more likely to trust themselves and others as adults, while those with insecure attachments often struggle with trust and being unable to identify or meet their own needs, and continue to abandon or betray themselves in adulthood by overcommitting or avoiding relationships. Whether secure or insecure, our earliest relationship patterns get wired into our subconscious minds, pulling us towards similar dynamics later in life. We'll explore this in a little while.

There is truth in this view, too: we're all connected at our core. No one is alone. At the deepest level, we're attached and we rely on each other. We exist together, not as isolated islands. Our life depends on the people and things around us. We all wish to feel this oneness down in our bones. Every person is a spiritual companion on this lifelong journey. Even when paths diverge, the bond remains at essence.

Throughout this book, unless I've said otherwise, I'm using 'attachment' in the spiritual sense of the term.

Attachment isn't limited to the way we attach ourselves to others. It's also about how we attach ourselves to the idea of how things should be. If you've made up your mind that love looks like gifts, shopping sprees and expensive trips every month, the person who instead offers you quality time, high-value conversation and emotional security won't feel like love. You're attached to the idea, not the person. Reality disappoints you.

When we cling to these stories, we fail to offer others and ourselves a chance to authentically show up to a connection. The stories we attach ourselves to are what rob of us of opportunities to let love show up in the expansive way it presents itself. The moment you insist your relationships must look a certain way, all other realities of it will cause distress and make you question if it's love at all.

Attachment is a double-edged sword – it is painful, though necessary. The spiritual and psychological perspectives on attachment both matter. When we can successfully integrate these views, we'll foster secure bonds while avoiding bondage. We'll have a healthy inner dialogue between love and attachment.

This is not an easy thing to do. It's hard to find that balance point.

To take love out of the box that attachments push it into, begin by understanding its unconditional and limitless nature.

Non-attached love in committed relationships

Romantic love beautifully reflects love's boundless essence between two souls. Yet unconditional love blooms most beautifully when it has no fences or limits. Between two people there is always give and take to work things out. Like when you and your partner argue over whether you should have pineapple on the pizza. You're still two separate people with your own quirky tastes, pet peeves and chaos. So romantic love has natural limits.

The beauty of lasting romance is that it accepts each person – pineapple pizza and all. It celebrates differences as much as commonalities. Rather than trying to change someone, true love says, 'I see you exactly as you are and choose you joyfully.'

When fully embraced, love makes even dull moments vivid. Life's richness reveals itself wherever we gaze, as if love turns life into high-definition. Previously blurry edges become sharp and clear.

How to maintain a bond without unhealthy clinging?

The spiritual view on non-attachment is not about giving up on people and possessions. It's about making sure those things don't possess you. 'The things you own end up owning you.' The problem isn't the object, it's the compulsive clinging attitude inside us. That's the shadow of the ego.

In a committed relationship, if we believe that we own our partner, ultimately, they will own us. We'll end up living in constant fear that they might slip from our grip. It's like grasping a metal pole with one arm while life pulls on your other arm, encouraging you to move on – the tension hurts, and the only way to alleviate the pain is to soften our hold.

The Buddhist teaching on impermanence reminds us that nothing in life remains the same forever. People come and go, moments pass by, and our body ages. The more we identify with these things, the more we suffer when these things change. When those temporary things fall away, it feels as if 'I' becomes smaller and weaker. But 'this too shall pass', as the saying goes.

Change is inevitable, as the Greek philosopher Heraclitus explained, making it the only constant. In truth, nothing is ever ours, because life is in a constant state of flux. Our bodies and thoughts, and even our dearly held beliefs, are also in flux. In fact, it is exactly this constant state of flowing change that makes life possible. Without this change there would be no life, and there could be no relationships either. Things would remain stuck and lifeless without change.

By acknowledging change, we cling less. Held lightly, bonds feel freer. Our journey together feels enriched when not gripped with fear.

Commitment in a relationship means you both promise to help the relationship grow and make an effort to keep it healthy. You look for ways to keep that promise alive in the face of changes, while remaining true to yourself and meeting your needs. And abiding by the rules you agreed to honour together, such as remaining monogamous.

If an unhealthy attachment occurs, the mind begins to cling to the person, which can lead to obsessive thinking about them, unrealistic expectations and reactive emotions when your needs aren't met. This clinging can manifest as possessiveness, jealousy, needing constant contact, monitoring their whereabouts and making your happiness dependent on their actions.

> *Your partner should support your happiness,*
> *not be the reason for it.*

When you get too attached, you start to see someone as yours, like they belong to you. This smothers the real closeness between you. It's hard to connect when you are trying to control. The inner focus is on the potential loss, rather than on the beauty and love of the relationship.

Letting go of control gives you both space to be yourselves. It allows each person the freedom to explore and be independent. This freedom lets relationships grow in healthy ways. This means letting go of another misconception – the myth of the binding contract.

Unconditional love
isn't a binding contract

*Sometimes, the discomfort we feel is an expression of
our unconditional love meeting people who only
want to love us conditionally.*

People often wonder why someone would choose to leave a romantic relationship when they have unconditional love for their partner. But to assume that love in a relationship means to commit to someone forever, despite how they behave, is to miss the point.

Love is not bound by time. Even though marriages are supposed to last 'until death do us part', some people change their minds. Others continue to love their partners long after their loved one has left their body. Many children who have lost parents and grandparents continue to love them after they are gone.

As we've seen, love isn't a contract with a due date or an expiry date. It has a timeless quality, and it exists in the present moment. I'd even suggest that love is presence.

It's essential to our understanding of love that we talk about it as truthfully as possible. If we are honest, we have to admit that no relationship is perfect. There are dull, difficult, uncomfortable and even painful things in the relationship – but the love that underpins the relationship is different.

Love is never 'bad'. It can't be. It is because we use the words 'love' and 'relationship' interchangeably that love gets a bad rap.

Even the phrase 'toxic love' is inaccurate: there is only toxic behaviour, which in turn creates unhealthy relationships; relationships that do not nurture authentic love.

A caution on conditions

Even though we commit to loving someone unconditionally, we can still recognize when *their* love comes with conditions and expectations.

While you might love another for who they are, they might only seem to love you based on what you can do for them. That suggests a fundamental mismatch in how you both feel and express love, indicating that the relationship may no longer be the right fit. Although the love you're giving is unconditional, the love you're receiving comes with conditions. To express that another way – the relationship you share is bound by conditions that don't fit the love in your core.

Or it might be the other way around – your love might have conditions, while your partner's is unconditional. Few of us like to admit this kind of thing, though.

Unconditional love is the foundation of all genuine connections. Expectations, boundaries and relationship rules are the house built upon it. The bones of the house are never more important than the foundation; they must be equally strong, healthy and reciprocated. You can't live in a home if the foundation is good but the structure built upon it is weak. When storms come, the structure will fall apart.

Remember, unconditional love extends spontaneously to everyone and all things. Relationships are a profound experience within that, and that's what requires sincere effort and hard work. It is meant to be a happy, cohesive experience. Unfortunately, many relationships exist without love. Loveless relationships are all structure and formula, with no real inner life. To be whole, a happy relationship needs that authentic spark from within, as well as the structure.

Loving with boundaries

Reciprocity is an essential part of any relationship. That means a healthy, fair give and take. Without it, one might question why people wouldn't simply remain single.

We choose relationships because they let us experience an exchange of energies and a broadening and deepening of our worldviews. It's not always a perfect 50–50 split, but neither is it a case of one person being the constant taker while the other person is the constant receiver. A relationship is not a charity.

We have the power to choose the relationships we want to nurture. In romantic relationships, some people might use the concept of 'unconditional love' as a cover to stay in a situation where there is no reciprocity.

While it might look like selfless behaviour, using unconditional love as the reason to stay in a relationship that doesn't provide a fair exchange of love is actually self-serving. It is often driven by someone's fear of being alone or by a desire to fulfil, with their partner, the parental love and acceptance they never had as a child.

A deep psychological need for acceptance might masquerade as love, but unconditional love is simply a boundless energy that we share in the present moment.

As we've already established, love can exist outside of a relationship and has little to do with another person at all. You can never offer someone love that you can't reach inside yourself. Therefore, love and relationships are not synonymous.

Love might be boundless energy, but human beings have limits, so our relationships must have boundaries that we stick to, in order to protect our time, space and energy. We must clearly communicate our needs and expectations for the sake of the relationship and to make sure our unconditional love doesn't encourage unconditional tolerance.

The unconditional love is at the centre of the ball – at the centre of our being. Conditions are only necessary on the surface of the ball – in the relationship. Keep that distinction clear, and you dissolve the myth of unconditional love as a binding contract.

We don't fall in love, we rise in love

I prefer to call it 'rising in love' rather than 'falling', as we soar to new heights of our potential within a warm, loving relationship.

If love is a state of being, the idea of 'falling in love' isn't quite accurate.

Love isn't something outside of us that we 'fall into'. Love is within all of us already. It's an ever-present energy towards which we rise up, and that also rises up within us. It's not a hole into which we fall.

The idea that love randomly happens to us, like an accident, or like getting struck by lightning, doesn't make sense.

'Falling in love' sounds as if love comes out of nowhere and just sweeps us away. Yet love has been here since the dawn of time. It is woven into our existence. Love has its home in the central, simple joy of just being what we are, as we are. Love was here before us and it will remain when we're gone.

Love isn't limited to romance, friendship or kinship. It is the magnet within each being that pulls us towards each other and towards life in the natural world around us. Authentic love starts as a seed-like quality inside us, and then develops, growing like a strong tree, as we choose to actively express and share it.

The more we cultivate the fundamental essence of love inside us, the more we recognize it in other people. We can nurture it and open it up so much that we begin to see it mirrored in everything, all the time.

The energy of love has an uplifting effect on us. It builds up inside, over time, as we become open to giving and to receiving love. It begins to rise in us like the approach of warm weather after a cold winter. Love brings a warmth into our world, and that warmth radiates outwards, uplifting those around us too. It's a 'rising' feeling.

When we meet 'the one', we go spiralling in a whirlwind of emotions, and the pull seems irresistible. It's like all our free will goes out of the window. The word 'falling' might seem to fit, but it describes the first rush of emotions, not the love itself. Our inner defences fall away. Our power of critical judgement falls to a low point. Our other life priorities fall from their place at the top of the list. Our need for friends falls away too. We only have eyes for one person.

You could say we go into freefall, not caring where we land, and often without a parachute. This is the idealized image of love – one where many people get stuck.

When relationships inevitably settle into something more mundane, or when our partner can no longer provide the same ecstatic feelings, we feel disappointed or restless, and we move on.

'Falling' makes it seem like we hurtle towards a painful crash, uncontrollably, without reason and objectivity – and that's why we so often hear that love hurts.

That is the reality in many love relationships, but we can avoid this desperate rush towards disaster if we understand the nature of love, and if we walk wisely in its light.

When we already have a secure connection to love within us, we won't long for it so desperately from another human being. We will still be able to share it, and enjoy receiving it – but without losing our heads completely. Allow me to illustrate what I mean.

Consider air. We don't talk about it much, but the moment we're underwater for too long, its value becomes obvious. The next breath is the only thing on our mind. Similarly, when we starve ourselves of self-love, we frantically cast about for it, and we will accept it from the first person to offer it to us.

A desperate pursuit of love only happens when we ignore the love for ourselves. If we don't have a secure connection to love, we end up gasping for a breath of air – a breath of love – and we feel as if we're drowning in loneliness. The moment we get the opportunity, we can't help ourselves. We gulp in as much as we can. When we finally get a gasp of fresh air – love from another person that we mistake for oxygen – that love feels far more valuable than it actually is.

Why limit the experience of love to a brief pocket of oxygen when you could be filling your lungs with pure, fresh air all of the time?

Infatuation is passive, love is active

The fiery passion at the beginning of a relationship is a wonderful experience, but replacing 'falling in love' with 'rising in love' shifts our mindset from a passive process that makes us vulnerable, to an active process that empowers the experience and the connection.

Rising in love emphasizes the growth and discovery within oneself and with a partner.

Falling in love emphasizes addictive emotional highs and potential ownership over another.

Rising in love manifests as continual daily actions that nurture intimacy. It shows up as curiosity about the other person, who is expanding and blossoming with us. It stretches beyond euphoric feelings to the divine celebration of a counterpart.

Higher perspectives open as we rise. The breathtaking view quiets our minds. We sit contentedly, hands linked, taking in how far we've come. Before tackling the next stretch, we secure our bond for the shared adventure ahead. We understand the shape of the mountain and know each other's abilities and weaknesses. We mindfully tend to our relationship roadmap, ensuring we have a shared trajectory. Using our inner self-love as a compass, we pave new trails, reach new heights and experience the beauty that lives within ourselves, each other, and the world around us.

Rising in love happens gradually, and consciously, with mutual trust anchoring both of you to the limitless opportunities that become available to experience unconditional love. That, in turn, attracts even more love into our lives.

Love attracts love

As you begin to discover love within yourself, your life improves. You start projecting a new vibe, at a higher frequency. You not only feel better, but blessings start to manifest in your life, like loving relationships.

Objects that are in synchronized vibration resonate with each other. Hit exactly the right note, and a fine wine glass begins to ring. 'Resonance' also occurs between the inner worlds of people.

When you're directly connected to your own [genuine] love, that *resonates* with other people who have the same quality. The inverse is also true: a surface-level connection to your own love, or a poor connection with a 'bad signal', will attract the same in another. The kind of love we radiate attracts, amplifies and reinforces the same kind of love from outside. This is a law of nature.

'You are not a drop in the ocean;
*you are the entire ocean in a drop.' – **Rumi***

A wave is made of water. The wave and water are not separate things, even though we use different words to identify them. A wave is just a moving form of water. Water can exist without the wave; but the wave cannot exist without the water.

This isn't just a metaphor, it is also a glimpse into the real nature of things.

Water represents the fundamental essence, or 'material', from which things are made. It represents the centre of our being's energy. The waves represent all the different individual forms and objects that arise from this essence.

Waves may look like separate individual things, but they are all unified at their source. All of water's forms – waves, spray, vapour, steam, ice and so on – are connected. They are simply different forms, different manifestations, of one substance.

Similarly, everything in this world is an expression of one existence, and one love. The loving source of life is what manifests as every living thing.

We are taught to think of ourselves as separate. We are made to feel like isolated, disconnected beings. We feel lonely in this vast Universe. We long for connection. As we've seen, this happens because of the constant conditioning and brainwashing that creates the ego. It is the ego that feels lonely, because the ego doesn't come from the source. It is something we acquire as we grow up, and something we have to defend all the time, otherwise it disappears.

When we return to love, all of that changes. Love sees no essential difference between self and other. On the surface we are different and unique, yes, but at the centre we are connected.

Love is a vibe

Just as love is who we are, love is the essential nature of everything else, too. Seeing this truth, we begin to see ourselves in a world of interesting connections.

We also start to notice those who are disconnected. We notice those who act from their fear-driven programming, rather than from love. This means we can take it less personally when people act in an unloving way towards us.

Being in a state of love helps us better connect to love in the world around us. Love attracts love. Love resonates with love, and is less affected by fear. The fear doesn't resonate as clearly.

It's like tuning an inner radio. We have to tune our inner dial to the love frequency to hear that channel clearly. Feeling love inside us tunes us into the love outside of us too.

Loving awareness becomes our constant broadcast. We attract others on our wavelength, because matched frequencies amplify one another. We start speaking the same body language of acceptance, even if we speak different languages or come from different backgrounds.

This isn't to say that our vibes can't influence another person's vibes when they aren't tuned to the same station. Love will certainly do that, and some people will be drawn to you even if they do not resonate with your frequency, simply because they want to experience the sounds you emanate.

Nevertheless, we choose romantic relationships with the intention to find a match, or at least a close fit – not to find someone to save or rescue. We can continue to brighten other people's lives by tuning into love without committing to a relationship with them.

The Law of Vibration, which I talked about in *Good Vibes, Good Life*, explains how like attracts like. It states that the energy that courses through you and radiates out into the world is the same energy that you welcome back. This is why exuding and nurturing positive vibes is so beneficial. It's all about selecting the right frequency, and staying there.

Tuning into the love frequency

To help you tune into the love frequency, here are eight easy practices from my own life that you could incorporate in yours.

1. Go for a walk and look for hearts – for example, heart-shaped rocks or leaves.

2. Repeat positive affirmations in front of a mirror, such as, 'I am beautiful, strong and resilient.'

3. Find one thing that you admire about every person you see throughout the day – it could be the way a stranger's smile radiates warmth.

4. Listen to uplifting songs and listen out for the word love. Or listen to solfeggio frequencies, which are said to provide a significant boost of love and positivity. According to some, the love frequency 528 Hz transforms our state of being, and 639 Hz has the ability to help us reconnect because it allows for introspection. You can find some for free on *The Rising Circle* YouTube channel, along with guided meditations.

5. Close your eyes and visualize giving someone you love a tight hug. Take note of what they're wearing. Notice how it feels; how they feel. What do they smell like? Can you hear them breathing? Are there any thoughts about love and joy going through your head?

6. Create. Art, in the form of writing, painting, dancing, singing and making music, can all be expressions of pure love.

7. Consume high-vibrational media. In other words, content that's uplifting, positive, inspiring, thoughtful or promotes personal growth. You are likely to ruminate on what you see on the TV, on social media and in books. These external influences affect your frequency.

8. Wish people well or pray for them. In Buddhism, the idea of metta, or loving kindness, is the heartfelt wish for the well-being of yourself and others. It's an outlook on life that you can cultivate by practising compassion for those around you.

You deserve a relationship where you are seen, heard, understood and accepted for who you really are.

PART TWO

First Connections

Get to know yourself first

The truth is, it is virtually impossible to build a healthy relationship with another person if you haven't built one with yourself first.

Getting to know yourself deeply will invite more conscious, happy relationships. Without understanding your core values and beliefs, relationships feel confusing and unstable. After all, how can you expect someone to get to know you if you don't know yourself – and how can you know them?

Once we know ourselves, we can accept ourselves and others.

Both self-awareness and self-love allow you to experience love and relationships in their greatest capacity. They not only help you identify relationships that reflect the love you give yourself, they allow you to see others in an unconditional light rather than through judgements.

When you let go of limiting ego stories about who you are, space opens up for love, compassion and wisdom to unfold within.

Truly knowing and loving yourself empowers your connections. We embrace ourselves, then we expand that embracing attitude towards others.

It pays to know your past patterns

In Eastern thought, you'll find the notion of 'samskaras', which are like psychological or emotional imprints left by everything that has ever happened to us in the past. It's these imprints that influence our behaviour, although we aren't usually aware of them.

The word samskara comes from the Sanskrit *sam* (meaning 'complete' or 'joined together') and *kara* (meaning 'action', 'cause' or 'doing'). Samskaras are said to be at the root of our character traits, impulses and ways of viewing the world.

Each individual impression, or samskara, is made up of ideas, beliefs and actions that condition us to behave in a particular way. The more often we repeat that conditioning, the deeper these impressions become, like a hammer driving in a nail, securing the conditioning.

The samskaras might be helpful or harmful. While carrying out helpful acts leads us to a sense of fulfilment, harmful ones block our journey. It's like continuously repeating the same mistakes, without stopping to really look at where you are going wrong. We can think of them as footpaths that form in nature when people and animals walk the same routes over and over again. The ground gets stamped down and the plants don't grow there. Then, because there's already a path, more animals and people use the same route, and the path becomes more defined. But this can change. If we stop using that path, over time it will disappear back into the landscape, as if it were never there.

Instead of wondering, 'Why does this keep happening?', reflect on repeated thoughts and patterns that are giving you the same unwanted results.

Think of your mind as a house with many rooms. In this house, the living room is your conscious mind and the basement is your subconscious or unconscious mind. The basement is where you store past experiences. It's likely you have a lot of forgotten memories down there – and while they might be forgotten, they haven't gone away.

You could say that samskaras ripple through our being like a thought wave, and the wave settles into our subconscious or unconscious mind. Anything that triggers a particular memory also triggers the samskara, which rises to your conscious mind, accompanied by all of the emotions associated with that memory. At the same time, you might block feelings that are too intense, preventing them from entering into your living area.

It's often those embedded experiences that make us act or feel the way we do, which is why self-awareness is so important. When you understand what triggers you, you can act more mindfully. Whatever is stored in your deeper unconscious mind can be changed when you bring it out into the open, because your present experiences are always changing.

Samskaras are like an X marked out on a map. Each X indicates our most fundamental perspectives and can be the key to identifying what we treasure most – and what inner patterns call for more tenderness and healing.

Can you recall an event that shaped you? Some of the less pleasant ones may even be blocked, as the mind tends to do this to protect us. For those out-of-reach memories, ask yourself: what topics or memories trigger intense discomfort when I talk about them? These are potentially related to a past trauma. What wounds still seek healing?

Perhaps you've noticed that it's hard to give and receive love. This is the case for many who were denied love for so long. It can be hard to find something when you have very little idea of what it looks or feels like. After all, the past has a peculiar way of shaping how we perceive life now.

Those of us who have had a series of unsuccessful relationships, or have witnessed dysfunctional connections, often lack a belief in love and the joy it can bring, and may equate it to stress and sadness.

Those who have been cheated on often fear sharing love and will block any attempts in the future, even when love naturally arises, to prevent themselves from getting hurt again.

You'll never reach a new destination if you keep walking the same route.

If you find it hard to give love, it might also be because you don't see its value. You may not directly associate giving love with happiness. Perhaps you've experienced love being weaponized against you – used as emotional blackmail, or manipulation. Or your vulnerability being used to shame you.

If you find it hard to receive love, it might be because you feel unworthy of it. This may come from early messages that implied you were somehow defective, or from experiences where others failed to make you feel cared for and appreciated.

Unlocking these emotional imprints can be as simple as tuning in. For many, this looks like meditation, journaling, therapy or taking a long walk. But all you need is the intent for self-discovery and some time and space to explore your patterns and seek to dissolve the beliefs that support them. It takes time, it takes practice and it requires the courage to be honest with yourself, but it remains one of the most powerful things you can do for yourself and your relationships.

As you unfold the samskaras, you won't have to guess what needs addressing. Focus on anything that hinders your ability to connect with yourself and others, and your intrinsic desire to love and be loved. You must let go of whatever stands in the way. The following chapters will show you how.

Those who are comfortable being alone can often love deeply and purely, because they are not sharing to receive, but simply giving.

Self-love brings you closer to who you are

*Self-love is doing what we need
to do to feel whole again.*

When our cup feels full on the inside, we're able to give so much more to the world around us – with vibrancy and clarity.

We can think of authentic self-love as the daily promise to prioritize our mind, body and spiritual well-being, in whatever way that presents itself.

Self-love might look like:

- Resting.
- Hitting the gym.
- Visiting a therapist.
- Following a passion.
- Working with purpose.

- Giving the house a clean.

- Addressing a harmful habit.

- Repeating positive affirmations.

- Dancing, singing or creating art.

- Journaling feelings and thoughts.

- Donating time or resources to help others.

- Unplugging from technology and social media.

- Reconnecting with neglected hobbies and interests.

These things may not necessarily feel comfortable at first, but by doing them, we can return to a feeling of wholeness that we might have otherwise avoided. Wants and needs are not the same things.

I like to call this self-love with a small 's'.

There are two types of self-love; there is also a big-'S' Self-love, as mentioned in Part One. This can be a little harder to achieve.

Big-'S' Self-love

Big-'S' Self-love happens in spontaneous moments of connection. It also happens through deliberate effort to access inner silence, for example, by meditating. So small-'s' self-love can help lead the way to it.

You are not your thoughts, emotions, dreams or body, you are the awareness that is experiencing all of them, which we can call the true Self. (Big 'S'.)

In Hinduism, the concept of the atman, or true Self, is fundamental. The atman refers to the eternal, unchanging 'I' within each living being – some people call it the soul or spirit. To realize this Self is to know love, and to know love is to love oneself. That's what I mean by big-'S' Self-love, and it's the purest love that exists. It's what we were talking about with the illustration of the ball. The true Self is the centre point; the small-'s' self is what forms on the outside of the ball.

When we touch the atman, we connect with the wellspring of authentic love inside. We become vessels through which this pure love can flow out and touch others. It lights us up with inner knowing and wisdom, and it elicits a feeling of deep connection to all beings.

These moments of realizing the atman are like mini-awakenings, where we profoundly understand our interconnectedness. Zen Buddhism describes similar sparks of enlightenment illuminating our path with the Japanese word 'satori'.

Imagine you've been listening to a radio station your entire life. It's familiar, though often filled with noise and static. You've never known any other station. One day, you turn the dial and a new station comes in, crystal clear. The music is stunning – rich, resonant, uplifting. It feels strangely familiar, like you've heard it before in a dream. You tune in again the next day, but you can't find that magical station. You realize it comes in faintly at times, but it keeps getting drowned out by your habitual station.

Over time, you learn to keep adjusting your inner radio dial until you tune back into that clear signal, even if just for a few moments. Gradually, you listen less and less to the static station you're used to. You've discovered a new frequency – the station of your true Self – and it's changing everything you hear. Though you can't yet stay tuned in 24/7, once you've had a taste, your ears have awakened.

This new inner station plays the music of your soul. Instead of exhausting noise, it fills you with energy. Like remembering a long-forgotten song, it feels welcoming and familiar. You start noticing this same music playing all around you, in others and in nature too. You realize the signal has always been there, waiting for you to discover it. Your life has just been tuned to the wrong station.

This turning of your inner dial – learning to access the station of the Self within – represents a spiritual awakening. Once accessed, it transmits a frequency of love that clears away static and opens your ears. The music of your true essence. The song of love.

When you realize your essence is love, it transforms how you see everything. You start perceiving the world through the lens of love. You notice love radiating all around you – even from other people – when before it may have felt hidden. It's like suddenly gaining X-ray vision to see everyone's loving and kind heart beating, regardless of the grumpy 'keep away' sweatshirt they might be wearing.

Although Self-love will help us to love other people wholeheartedly, loving ourselves, especially at this deepest level, is something that ebbs and flows throughout life; some days will be harder than others. Self-love is a lifelong journey of tuning back into the love frequency.

A meditation practice for Self-love

One of the most effective ways to discover the Self is through practices like meditation.

Our minds are like screens displaying action movies, which we mistake for our true selves. Meditation gives us an opportunity to turn off the screen and experience pure awareness, which unearths a connection with your true Self.

When we sit down to meditate, hidden emotions and impulses begin to reveal themselves to us. Why is this? During waking hours, your mind is distracted by a million other things – media, work, friends, family responsibilities, entertainment, keeping the cat away from the fish tank. When you're constantly thinking and analyzing, you can't be conscious of what's lurking in the deep sea of your mind.

It is only when you sit in quiet, and with focus, that your memories, fears, desires and hopes start to rise to the surface. When you make a gap in your mind by being still, the contents of your unconscious mind start to rise up for you to become conscious of them. As a result, meditation can feel challenging and offputting at first. But with regular practice, it tends to become easier and more comfortable as you build familiarity. Be patient with yourself through the friction phase – the peace you will find on the other side makes it worth sticking at.

There is a technique that I find simple enough to keep trying, and powerful enough to cultivate silence quickly, without much experience at all.

The practice is called Hakalau, which is an ancient Hawaiian tradition practised by the Huna or Hawaiian spiritual teachers and martial artists – you could call them Polynesian Shamans. Hakalau translates to 'eyes wide open', but it refers to the mind's eye rather than your physical eyes.

Hakalau meditation

When we practise Hakalau, we focus on a fixed point with a softened gaze, while allowing the rest of our surroundings, objects and sensations to enter through peripheral vision and be in our awareness. Doing this calms our nervous systems.

Start by focusing for a few minutes at a time, then gradually increase the duration as you become more comfortable with the practice.

Here are the steps – for the purpose of this exercise, I've varied the instructions slightly from the standard Hakalau practice. Give yourself a chance to get familiar with these before trying this practice for the first time.

1. Choose a quiet and comfortable place where you won't be disturbed. Avoid music or any other distractions. Sit or stand comfortably with a straight spine.

2. Close your eyes and take a few deep breaths to relax your body. Let go of any tension in your muscles and allow your body to settle into a comfortable and relaxed state.

3. Open your eyes but keep them soft and unfocused. Allow your gaze to be gentle and let your eyes rest on a point in front of you without staring directly at it. Imagine looking through or beyond the point.

4. While maintaining the soft gaze and keeping your eyes still, start to become aware of your peripheral vision. Allow your awareness to expand outwards – first left, then right, then up, and then down to the farthest parts of the space you're in, without straining your eyes. Take in the entire visual field around you. Notice the colours, shapes and movements in your periphery without directly focusing on them.

5. As you continue to breathe deeply, maintain a sense of relaxed awareness. Your attention is not fixed on any particular point; instead, it flows outward, embracing the entire field of vision.

6. If your mind starts to wander, or if you become distracted, gently bring your focus back to the soft gaze and the expansiveness of your peripheral vision. It's a practice that requires staying present in the current moment.

My hope is you will experience a sense of peaceful stillness and tranquillity. But don't worry if you don't feel this right away.

Whether you're new to meditating or you're a seasoned monk, the biggest challenge while doing it is finding and holding the silence. Try not to go in with the intention of achieving a particular state, but instead try to simply cultivate a more open awareness. And don't get frustrated if busy thoughts linger longer than you'd like. Your practice is still working, even when the effects aren't immediate.

You might be tempted to put a label on what you're experiencing. 'Am I experiencing something profound?' But using the mind to understand what is beyond it is a trap of the ego. Instead, just be with the presence.

While you're looking softly outwards, notice the heart of you. Each thought, each distraction will pull you outwards, away from your still, peaceful centre. Return again and again to the centre point, without force. No matter what thought or feeling appears to you, come back to that centre point, your own awareness. Turn your attention inwards, without analyzing – and get to know yourself directly.

Self-love isn't selfish

Self-love means checking in with ourselves regularly.
It means asking what we need in order to thrive,
without denying our experiences or emotions –
or anyone else's.

When misused, self-love becomes an excuse to fulfil cravings and boost our self-image without considering how our actions might impact others and the world around us. For example, we might use self-love as a reason to consume lots of junk food or see ourselves as superior to others. It's like telling yourself 'I'm worth it!' as justification to buy the overpriced shoes you can't actually afford when you really need new tyres for the car.

This false self-love keeps us trapped in our comfort zone or encourages us to make unintelligent decisions. While it may feed immediate desires, it doesn't necessarily provide fulfilment or nourishment. It's a poor substitute for the real thing.

Self-love is being kind and considerate towards oneself without intentionally being unkind and inconsiderate towards others. It nourishes all, from a place of balance. Selfishness grabs what it can, without a thought for anything or anyone else. It feeds the self but harms the environment around it. Self-love thinks of the end-game, while selfishness looks for instant satisfaction.

Authentic self-love isn't selfish because, at its root, there is compassion. When we're kind and patient with ourselves, it's easier to be understanding and generous with others too. We exercise self-love first, because we deserve a beautiful and loving connection with our inner being; and second, because it allows us to contribute powerfully to the rest of our relationships.

Self-love prioritizes your needs, values and intuition in everything you do. It unapologetically honours your well-being and the boundaries that are in place to protect it. It recognizes your worth, overcomes your inner critic and shapes how you perceive and experience life.

I sometimes see people excuse arrogant or rude behaviour in the name of self-love. If you're acting from that mindset, you probably don't love yourself very much. You're not comfortable and confident about your worthiness and your value, so you outwardly heighten it. You feel the need to wear a mask. You feel like you have to trick others into believing in you. It's a disguised form of people-pleasing.

Arrogance is an external performance; self-love is an internal experience. Arrogance is an attempt to manipulate how you relate to or are perceived by others; self-love nurtures and heals how you relate to yourself.

This isn't to say that self-love won't appear arrogant to some. When you are anchored to the truth of who you are, and, more deeply, the loving essence at your core, it's difficult to be manipulated or swayed by anyone who isn't coming from a place of love. You won't fall into traps or for hidden agendas, or give in to negative opinions, and ultimately, people might label their inability to control you as arrogance on your part.

Security and confidence may also irritate others who haven't discovered it for themselves. Others may become envious of the empowerment that exudes from those who love themselves. It is, after all, obvious and hard to miss.

Self-love begins with an understanding of who you are and honouring what you need. If you give in to another person just to please them, there's a chance that you'll sacrifice your own emotional well-being in favour of theirs. This can lead to resentment, which often leaks out as passive-aggressive behaviour.

Beyond people-pleasing, self-love also helps to shield you and your relationships from:

- Relationships where you give more than you receive.

- Taking on more work than you can handle, and the burnout that follows.

- Withholding self-expression and blocked creativity.

- Dependence on external validation.

- Anxiety-induced perfectionism.

- Comparison, jealousy and envy.

Rejecting self-love leads to self-betrayal

When we reject self-love by disregarding our intuition, values and needs, we are essentially betraying ourselves. Self-betrayal is choosing something that isn't choosing you. We might make a decision that doesn't serve our best interests, or keep someone with status around us because they could help us advance in our career, even if they mistreat us.

Self-betrayal looks like:

- Saying 'yes' when you want to say 'no'.

- Regularly putting the needs of others before your own.

- Compromising your values to keep others comfortable

- Performing to feel loved or wanted.

Self-betrayal encourages us to deprioritize our needs, suppress our feelings, hide aspects of ourselves, play a false character and overextend ourselves to keep others happy. It's an attempt to receive love and feel validated by denying what's true to you. It is ultimately self-defeating.

It becomes glaringly apparent that we've betrayed ourselves, because there's a sense of uneasiness, confusion, contempt, anxiety and resentment that results from our choices. Refusing to honour ourselves can also leave us feeling stuck, overwhelmed, helpless and exhausted. When we have cultivated the habit of being dishonest with ourselves, it's hard to break that habit and get real with ourselves again.

Of course, it can be tricky to approach. Serving others and caring for those who depend on us are essential factors in a functioning society and in healthy relationships. For example, caregiving requires sacrifice. Nearly any parent will tell you that they put their child's needs before their own.

Balanced care nourishes both self and others. You can't serve anyone when you're depleted. Even rescuer figures need respite from saving others. By rejecting our own needs, we betray our capacity to contribute meaningfully.

If you often feel drained after giving so much of yourself, then the need for self-love is far more critical. This calls for daily routines, habits and personal rituals to tend to your mind, body and spirit.

This was true for me, and something I had to learn and work on. What I often thought of as being considerate, a desire to see others happy, and a calling to make everyone around me feel good, eventually became an unconscious behaviour to extend myself even when I had nothing left to give.

I believed my people-pleasing habits were selfless, but really they were a subtle way of manipulating circumstances to protect myself from experiencing the negative feelings that might stem from rejection, or the awkwardness of setting a boundary. In other words, they were self-serving. The irony is that people-pleasing would lead to negative feelings anyway, because I was betraying myself in the process.

For instance, when I hosted get-togethers at my home, I would invite friends from my wider social circle because I wanted to make everyone feel included and have a good time together. Though these events took much time, money and energy to arrange, a part of me hoped that by including everyone, I would be seen as considerate and welcoming, and that people would continue to make an effort with me.

Over time, however, I noticed that I only saw some of these friends at my own gatherings. Otherwise, I'd never hear from them. Despite feeling hurt by their one-sided participation, I continued to welcome them warmly each time, afraid that excluding them would be seen as petty or rude, and encourage gossiping about me – something that would damage my giving and friendly self-image.

My overly inclusive guest list wasn't coming solely from generosity: it was fuelled by a hope that being accommodating now would inspire reciprocal generosity later. But this transactional dynamic only led to inauthentic relationships that were missing real care and connection.

While my intentions weren't ill-meaning, catering to inconsistent friends led to emotional fatigue and resentment on my end. And banking on returned invites kept me tethered to conditional giving with strings attached. I realized I needed to recalibrate, and to channel my efforts into nurturing authentic, mutually caring relationships.

The only person who knows if they're betraying themselves is you. And if you are betraying yourself to keep others happy, you will miss out on true connection.

Think of your favourite person in the world – someone you adore, respect and appreciate. How would you feel if they came to you and confessed that most of what they do and say is to make you feel good and not a reflection of how they truly feel or who they truly are?

You'd be crushed. You would either feel like the person is treating you like a charity case, or you would lose your respect for them as an authentic human being.

When you demonstrate people-pleasing tendencies, you're making assumptions about who others want you to be – when all they might be seeking is an honest connection with the most authentic version of yourself.

Do you know who
will never leave your side?

You.

Perhaps this is the relationship
you need to nurture the most.

Your 'type' isn't necessarily good for you

In romantic relationships, physical attraction might be important, but character is vital. Not everyone who's easy on the eye is great for your soul.

In today's Western societies, single people have – for the most part – freedom when it comes to choosing their partners. And with a plethora of dating apps where we can simply swipe right on anyone who catches our eye, options are plenty.

Sifting through the masses of fish in the sea who 'love hiking and laughing' leaves us both overwhelmed and underwhelmed. We second-guess if we should ditch dependable Dean for Declan's dreamy abs once the spark fizzles. Forget soulmates, we struggle to choose between tacos or ramen for dinner!

The paradox of choice has us chasing that Hollywood high. We feel entitled to 'the one' . . . who meets all 500 items on our manifesto, stays effortlessly gorgeous and laughs at our jokes. Meanwhile, we overlook gentle and sweet Niamh next door.

With so many choices, how do you make the right decision and not leave empty-handed or broken-hearted? You might be attracted to a lot of people, but is attraction on its own enough to sustain a relationship? And when you find different people attractive for different reasons, how do you know who is right for you?

What is attraction for you?

'Why do I always fall for the bad boys?'
'Why does every girl I'm with cheat on me?'

It can feel like we are victims of our attraction preferences. Truthfully, if you have a 'type', and that type repeatedly leads you down a path to heartache, what you have isn't a preference – it's a pattern of picking people who reflect the unhealed parts of you.

Attraction is mostly unconscious. Our desires are often driven by what we lacked early in life. We may also be motivated to seek partners who cause us to relive the trauma in hopes of unconsciously resolving it. This is why understanding our patterns is so important.

For instance, if we lacked affection in childhood, we might chase people who can't commit, as we try in vain to win the distant parent's unavailable love. Or, if we learned love as unpredictable highs and lows, 'exciting' volatility draws us in, but it can leave us feeling depleted when it inevitably comes to an end.

Those who perfectly fit an unconscious longing can seem like a worthy prize. But resisting this magnetic pull is sometimes the most loving act we can do for ourselves.

How to undo your conditioning – and start finding love in all the right places

Navigating your preferences beyond your conditioning is hard work, but so fun. Imagine only knowing about American pop artists, then discovering the range of global musical cultures, like K-pop and Bossa Nova.

It's astonishing how preferences expand when our hearts do. And when we begin seeking better alternatives, life reflects what we truly need and desire.

When you're considering a current or potential partner, first think about how they make you feel. When you're around them, can you be a relaxed and open version of yourself, or do you feel like you need to perform an act? Do you second-guess what you say and do, or can you simply be present in the moment with them?

Next, pay attention to how they treat people in varying contexts. Does their warmth remain consistent? How do they speak about previous partners or friends? Do they take responsibility for their past actions and decisions? Or do they find ways to put the blame on others?

Discuss what you both believe about love and sustaining emotional intimacy. Are your visions compatible or clashing? Your differences can be complementary, but your core needs must align.

Asking thoughtful and open-ended questions in the early stages of dating can help establish compatibility and foster a deeper connection. Here are some questions you can ask based on seven key relationship pillars.

The questions aren't a test for someone to pass or fail – they're a way of steering conversations to an honest and maybe even vulnerable place that allows you to connect. Feel free to take the spirit of a question and change the language to make it your own.

Mutual respect

- What does mutual respect mean to you in a relationship?
- Can you share an experience where you felt truly respected in a past relationship?

Aligned values and morals

- What are your top two or three values that you want to nurture in your life?
- How do you define what is morally right or wrong, and what influences your moral compass?

Good communication

- How do you tend to handle disagreements or conflicts with others?
- What does good communication in a relationship look like for you?

Physical attraction

- How important is physical attraction to you in a relationship?
- Can you describe what you find attractive in a person beyond physical appearance?

Empathy

- How do you typically show empathy to your partner during challenging times?
- What has empathy looked like for you in past relationships?

Shared relationship goals

- What are some of the ways we could support each other in being our best and healthiest selves?
- How do you envision your ideal partnership in terms of financial, emotional and spiritual goals?

Honesty and integrity

- How do you handle situations where honesty is difficult but necessary?

- Have you ever been in a situation where you felt your integrity was being tested? How did you handle it?

Remember, the key is not just asking the questions but actively listening to their responses and sharing your own thoughts and experiences. This will help build a foundation of trust and understanding between you.

Don't let perfect be the enemy of good

The modern love story wants it all: romance, sex, friendship, security, companionship, domesticity, respectability and material benefits.

That's a lot to hope for from one person, especially if you also expect your partner to be philosophical yet playful, subtle yet spontaneous, hilariously witty yet patiently listening. Oh, and a killer decorator with the singing voice of an angel. No pressure!

When you turn to a potential partner to fulfil all of your own needs, you risk overwhelming your relationship in the name of finding the perfect 'one'. You might also unconsciously be keeping one foot out of the door by prioritizing your search for 'the one' over being present with the one in front of you.

The truth is, even the most compatible partners will fall short sometimes. They, like you, are imperfect works in progress. But a good connection, with healthy communication and emotional availability, can become something great over time. Don't let perfect be the enemy of good. Invest in what you have built together rather than chasing phantoms.

We'll explore more later about how your childhood attachment patterns can affect your expectations and commitment readiness when seeking a partner. Unrealistic expectations driven by past hurts can sabotage an otherwise promising connection.

For now, know that your capacity to love relies on your ability to let go of fantasies and ground yourself in the real. The person wonderfully and imperfectly human sitting across from you deserves your full presence.

Love is not blind

*May you find a love that radically accepts the parts
of you that you're still working on.*

We've all heard the phrase 'love is blind', suggesting that love causes us to overlook less-desirable qualities in another person. But blind love doesn't actually exist.

How can you love someone when you can't see who they truly are?

Let's take Sarah and Mark as an example. They've been dating for a few months. In the beginning, Sarah put Mark on a pedestal – he seemed like the perfect guy. She would brag about how smart, handsome and successful he was. She loved telling her friends and family about him.

As time went on, Sarah started to notice Mark's flaws. He could be arrogant at times, distant on the weekends, and wasn't as motivated in his career as she had thought.

Sarah clung on to the fantasy version of him, the one for which she had fallen. Whenever he acted differently, she justified, ignored or simply hoped that he would eventually change.

She believed she loved him, but really, she loved the image of him that she had in her mind. It was an image based on his past actions; an image without flaws, an image of who he could become in the future. This image did not accept the man in front of her, it was created to meet her expectation of who that man *ought* to be.

As a result, Sarah tolerated unjust behaviours and cheated herself and Mark out of a fulfilling relationship. This is not her fault; she had learned to hold on to hope – a common coping mechanism for children who are given inconsistent affection while growing up.

The halo effect

We tend to assign positive attributes to people we find physically attractive. As a result, we might overlook incompatibilities or rationalize negative behaviours early in dating, before really getting to know the person.

There's a reason for this – it's known in psychology as the halo effect.

The halo effect is a cognitive bias that was first coined by psychologist Edward Thorndike in 1920. Thorndike put forward that when people have one likeable or desirable quality, we assume (without evidence) that they also possess other positive qualities.

Imagine you meet someone who's exceptionally good-looking. Or they might be impressive in another standout way – maybe they're a famous actor or a successful athlete. Because of this one positive attribute, you might unconsciously assume that they're also good in other areas of their life. It's as if their 'halo' of attractiveness or success casts a favourable light on everything about them, even things you don't know about yet. We're almost blinded by the light emitting from their halo, so much so that we can't see past it.

So, you might assume they're smart, kind and talented, just because they have that initial 'halo' of good looks or success. But in reality, they might have flaws or be just like anyone else. The halo effect is about how our first impression of someone can colour our perception of their overall character.

It can work in the opposite direction, too, where one negative trait leads us to perceive other traits more negatively.

When we have strong feelings for someone, it can skew our perceptions to focus only on their positive qualities. We might idealize partners and ignore signs of incompatibility under the halo effect.

If someone reminds us of a past love or caretaker, we associate those positive memories and transfer them onto the new person. Nostalgia creates an illusion of compatibility.

Seeing people for who they are

The unconditional love at the centre of our being is reached through honesty. The facades that people believe on the surface of life are full of deception and illusion.

To counteract the halo effect, try to view new partners objectively. Don't make excuses for them or justify incompatibilities or bad behaviours. Pay attention to any negativity you may be ignoring. Focus on truly getting to know the real person over time before making conclusions about compatibility or chemistry. Most importantly, listen to your intuition, and be deeply honest with yourself.

When we cling to an ideal image, we're blinded to the flaws that are emerging.

Consider your experiences with self-love. You begin with acceptance. Creating space for all aspects of your being, you open up and look into the darkest corners of your heart and welcome them into the light. You remain curious about what you'll find, knowing every part of you will be met with love. This is how we extend the same grace and compassion to everyone else. We open up the floor to them. We invite all of them to the stage. Not just the bits that seem presentable.

When we focus on idealized versions of people, we will attract inauthenticity. We unconsciously send out the message that we have not accepted our own broken parts and therefore reject that aspect in others.

Blind love seals us in fantasy, unable to see or respond to the reality of who someone is. We justify, explain and dream away real problems, protecting the perfect image of them that we have built up.

In doing so, we fail to truly know the person before us. Our love becomes conditional – contingent on them fulfilling our fantasy. Inevitably, reality breaks the spell, leaving us feeling disappointed when they act like human beings, not as the heroes in the picture we painted.

Mature love is informed by wisdom. It transforms infatuation into insight. With open eyes, we see another's whole humanity – light and shadow, strength and weakness. Despite their flaws, we care for their well-being, not just a romanticized notion of who they could be. With vision unclouded by illusion, we connect with what is genuine.

Love can only occur with open eyes and an open heart.

Psychological games get you played

When it's right, you'll both just know. No games, no guessing, no convincing. If you have to prove your worth, they aren't for you. Don't chase those who leave you feeling uncertain. Wait for the one who chooses you clearly and without hesitation.

For many, dating resembles a strategic game more than a search for connection. We craft clever profiles to showcase 'best selves', then swipe prospects like human Candy Crush.

If someone shows interest in us, little power games start happening. One person might not text back for a few days, acting aloof to seem hard to get. The other might reply unpredictably to keep you hooked. Each reply is like a small 'win' for the person on the receiving end, giving them a rush of dopamine and leaving them craving more. It's like we're playing mental slot machines, pulling the lever each time we send a text to see if we'll hit the jackpot of reciprocated interest. And around and around it goes, as we try to keep the excitement of potential connections alive.

Each person tries to gain leverage while acting like they don't care. A part of this dance is a harmless and entertaining leftover from our biological ancestry; many species of animals and birds play these games too. With humans, it gets terribly complicated when our emotions are caught up in ego games.

What do you 'win' from these sly moves?

For instance, how many of us have been left questioning our worth after receiving someone's silence?

> *You leave a welcome mat out*
> *in front of your heart for somebody who*
> *doesn't want to enter, then conclude that*
> *something's wrong with your house.*

This feeling of incompleteness may come from something as small as not receiving a text back. Imagine you meet someone at a bar and identify them as a potential love interest. The next day, you send them a text saying:

> *Hey, it's me from the bar last night. Was lovely meeting you. I thought I was staying in but my friends managed to drag me out, lol. Anyway, it was a good night in the end because we had a laugh with you guys. Hope you had fun too?*

A week goes by, and you still haven't heard back. As you wait, your mind might identify yourself as not good enough, purely because they haven't shown you immediate interest. Days later, you get a text back from them and it reads:

Sorry for the late reply, been really busy. Was good meeting you too. Hope you're good. What have you been up to?

Although it's brief and they don't tell you why they were busy, it seems like they're still interested in you. So you reply to them within a day, but this time you put more effort into your message so you can get a conversation going.

Again, you don't hear back from them for another week. This time their reply is even briefer than the last one, and it includes no questions back to you:

That's cool, hope you had fun. Yeah, I've just been busy with stuff. Can't wait for the weekend.

You might decide to play it cool and reply back a week later because this has become a game – one in which you're both playing hard to get. You've accepted that it's OK to toy with each other's emotions, so you invite yourself to get played some more. Or you might choose to reply quickly, as you have been doing all along. But now you're worried that you look desperate.

In relationship games, everyone loses

With both approaches, you're self-sabotaging. You've lowered your self-esteem and set the tone for your future with this person. You might find yourself constantly submitting through people-pleasing, just to feel worthy of receiving love.

Although anticipation can create excitement, games imply winners and losers.

There might be challenges to overcome in the early stages of a healthy relationship, such as a fear of vulnerability. This is common because being real with someone is scary. Taking off our masks risks revealing parts we think are flawed or unwanted. What if sharing our whole self drives them away? This might encourage someone to push away a prospective lover if they get too close, or play a game where they subtly test if someone is safe to be authentic around. Can I trust you yet? Will the real version of me weird you out or draw you closer?

But with disguises on, we can't discover genuine compatibility. Without tough and honest conversations, our relationships are fragile and surface-level. Psychological games deliver distance and destroy true intimacy.

The patterns we set up in the beginning shape the dynamic of the relationship throughout. These can be hard to shift when they are firmly in place. For this reason, healthy relationships rarely start with deliberate games.

It's our ego-self that feels driven to manipulate and control people and situations. This controlling urge comes from inner tension and fear all tangled up with the false ego-identity.

As a way to manage these anxieties, the ego wages subtle power games in relationships. It sees love as a battlefield to 'win' instead of something to mutually give and receive.

But our essence underneath the ego lies untouched by any of that drama. Our core Self remains peaceful, not needing to grasp at or change anyone. It is happy to remain quietly in the centre, beaming out love.

The surest sign that you're on the right track with someone is when both your connection and communication are easy and natural – not forced or purposely delayed.

Dealing with ghosts

In a generation where it's easier to run away,
ghost someone or swipe to the next person, appreciate
those who stay, communicate how they feel
and are willing to fix things.

'Ghosting', or vanishing from someone's life without a word, is the ultimate dating horror-flick drama. One day your snuggle buddy is raving about how the Universe brought you together . . .

the next – *poof* – they've pulled a Houdini on you, no explanation. Now, you've been left on read.

It's impossible to spot a future ghost. They seem so open and honest over pizza bagels on the couch, tracing your palm lines and talking destiny. Then the next thing you know, you're left hovering in the empty chat void.

But the reason for ghosting is pretty straightforward. The person disappearing without a word is too uncomfortable to say why, leaving the ghosted person to solve the puzzle alone.

If you've been the victim of this act, it's important to understand this: the person who ghosts you is doing you a favour. They aren't capable of or willing to communicate big emotions, manage confrontation or exercise authenticity. Had they stayed, an intimate connection or genuine friendship would've been impossible to foster.

How to cope when someone disappears

Getting ghosted can leave you confused, shocked and hurt. Here are some tools to navigate this confusing time, so you can return to fearlessly loving someone new.

- Acknowledge your emotions and practise self-compassion. First, honour your feelings. You are allowed to feel angry and heartbroken. These emotions are messengers guiding you towards inner healing. Accept them so you can release them.

- Seek support. Connect with trusted friends or a therapist who can provide a listening ear and offer insights. Sharing your experiences can be profoundly healing.

- Reflect and learn. Use this experience as an opportunity for self-discovery. Reflect on what you want from your relationships and how you can grow from this encounter.

- Forgive and release. Holding on to anger and resentment only hinders your healing journey. Choose to forgive the person who ghosted you, not for their sake but for your own inner peace. More on this later.

- Reconnect with the energy you lost. Whether through prayer, meditation or mindfulness, reconnect with your values and relationship intentions. Don't allow someone's actions to question whether you've taken improper steps to connect.

How to stop playing the game

If people are unwilling to show you the respect and attention you deserve, there's no need to beg. You can't force a connection that's only coming from one side. And if you've done inner healing work and you actively exercise self-love, you'll know where your heart feels welcomed and safe. But there may be some pitfalls that even the most self-aware of us could miss.

Be cautious of those who are only ready to connect with you when it's convenient for them or when they are lonely. Consistent effort is usually the most significant indicator of genuine interest.

But do keep other people's well-being in mind – some people may want to reply but can't due to commitments and priorities. Your intuition (not to be confused with trauma or fear) can help indicate whether or not someone is genuinely interested in you. Intuition is a clear and calm sense of knowing that is derived without logical reason. There are no anxieties or paranoia obstructing it. When intuition arrives, the body is comfortable, even if the truth in the message isn't.

Remember, if it's transparency you want, transparency you must offer. Lay your cards on the table and be gently upfront about your needs. This isn't a to-do list that you hand someone, it's a vulnerable discussion that offers them insight on what you hope to experience with them. Always stay true to yourself, though, and only compromise as much as you feel comfortable.

Many suppress their needs in order to be seen as 'chill' or to be liked. This is actually manipulation. It's unfair to blame or punish someone for not giving you what you never asked for. Ultimately, denying authentic desires slowly drains the life energy from you. You deserve a partner who honours your reasonable non-negotiable needs without shaming you for having them. That isn't entitlement – it's reclaiming wholeness.

The right person for you is the one who loves you the way you are and doesn't ask you to change anything about yourself. Who wouldn't want that?

And you're only the right person for them if you don't expect them to be someone else, either. If you want your new partner to change, you aren't with the person that you wanted to be with in the first place, and nor are they.

Once we're engaging in relationships from a place of sincerity, the warning signs about potential partners will be much easier to see.

We all have some red-flag behaviours

*Everyone has some 'red-flag' behaviours,
because we've all been hurt in the past.
Nevertheless, notice those who are committed to
learning and growing, and those who are OK with
blaming everyone else. Some take responsibility
and remain accountable, while others believe
that they're fine the way they are.*

Red flags were historically used in war to indicate danger. In relationships and dating, we use the term to talk about warning signs in the behaviour of the person we're seeing – behaviour that might suggest future problems. Patterns like control, unpredict-ability, dishonesty or disrespect that can undermine intimacy.

You can learn a lot about someone from how they describe their life journey. How empowered, responsible and accountable are they for their experiences? Or do you get the sense that they blame the world for conspiring against them?

Sometimes, the beliefs and defences that come from our most painful experiences can trap the pain within and manifest as red flags when someone gets too close. These reflexive self-protection behaviours shout, 'Proceed with caution!', because you have unhealed wounds. They suggest that connecting and holding space with you may prove challenging.

You can only venture so far with people who are unwilling to grow. Defensiveness sets limits on mutual understanding and learning. Cue scenarios where buried wounds ignite into drama with the slightest friction.

How to deal with red flags – theirs and ours

In whatever way they appear, we all have at least a few red flags. But an awareness of them brings them into the light and creates opportunities to tend to and heal unhealthy beliefs and behaviours. Awareness means consciously recognizing automatic reactions rooted in old wounds. Though instincts arise before we can think, awareness creates a space between impulse and response. Within this gap, choice becomes possible. We no longer have to act from old defences alone.

Whereas building walls around your troublesome tendencies can make you emotionally reactionary, hard to get close to and challenging to grow beside.

You might truly yearn for stability, yet keep rocking the boat with your volatile outbursts or inconsistent behaviour.

If you feel unworthy of love, you may unconsciously reject it by forcing the relationship to break down.

If you consider yourself growth-minded, aware of your red flags and someone who takes responsibility for their healing, here's the best thing you can do for someone who isn't. You can demonstrate taking accountability for your life and share how empowering it is to know you can choose how you experience the world and the beautiful, multi-faceted individuals who occupy it.

Red flags or not, we are all loveable and we all deserve compassion and understanding. And there's no need to judge others, regardless of their level of consciousness and self-awareness. We cannot convince each other of the importance of growth; we can only love others so that they may see they deserve the peace and power that comes with it.

The gift of grace

With patience, love and compassion, we understand why we are the way we are. After all, we know we're much better than we used to be. And yet, it seems much harder to extend the same amount of grace to others.

The idea of a red flag simply reminds you that someone is human. They have a tremendous capacity for imperfection. But the label itself is condemning and unforgiving and suggests isolating someone because they don't share the same level of awareness as you.

This isn't to say you overlook mistreatment, tolerate a lack of growth or even engage with someone who lacks development. But at the very least, we don't mark them with a scarlet letter.

Allow others the grace you hope to be shown yourself. That non-judgemental, unconditional space is a healing capacity we can create for others.

Use these prompts to journal or dive deeper into how you can reconstruct your beliefs about red flags.

- Think of someone in your life who may be displaying red flags. How can you actively listen and empathize with their struggles rather than jump to conclusions?

- Consider the concept of 'assuming positive intent' when faced with red flags. If you accept that everyone is simply trying their best with the tools they have, how might your interactions become more compassionate?

- Reflect on the idea that everyone is navigating their own journey, complete with flaws and scars. How can you embrace the imperfections in others with an open heart?

Secure attachments never go out of style

When you offer someone safety and security,
you guide their nervous system towards
love rather than fear. You gift their body ease,
so they can be present – and show up
as exactly who they are.

Our childhood memories may be hazy or blocked altogether. Psychologists describe 'attachment issues' arising early on, but these can be difficult to spot in ourselves. That's why it's difficult to know why we act the way we do as adults. Many common struggles – like jealousy, control issues or conflicts – trace back to our attachment patterns from childhood.

You likely have ingrained assumptions about how a partner should treat you, and vice versa. If these are habitual patterns, they could stunt the relationship from the start. Sometimes, we just can't understand why we don't feel fulfilled in our relationships, but attachment styles provide us with a clue.

During our first years, attachment styles form in response to the type of bonds we create with our parents or caregivers. We unconsciously learn to what degree we can trust and count on nurturing when we need comfort. This becomes a blueprint for our ability to attach intimately once we become adults.

According to attachment theory, there are four different attachment styles:

Secure Attachment

'I feel comfortable being close to my partner, and I trust that they care about me. We can talk openly about our feelings.'

This style develops from an environment where children were made to feel consistently loved, safe and cared for by parents or caregivers. Secure attachment looks like:

- Having a healthy, trusting and comfortable stance towards intimacy.
- Feeling at ease with both closeness and independence in relationships.
- Trusting that your partner cares about you and that you can talk openly about feelings together.
- Having healthy responses and coping mechanisms for relationship conflict.

Anxious Attachment

'I constantly need reassurance from my partner that they love me and won't leave. I worry when they're not with me.'

An anxious attachment style often links to inconsistent early care, where the child's needs were sometimes met, but unpredictably so. It looks like:

- A fear of abandonment and a constant need for reassurance.

- Worrying continually about your partner's feelings and commitment to the relationship.

- Needing ongoing validation that your partner cares and won't leave – and feeling anxious when you're apart.

- Feeling jealous or finding it hard to trust your partner.

- When conflicts arise, clinging to your partner more tightly in fear of them leaving, even if that means forgoing your own needs for the sake of the relationship.

If you recognize these characteristics in yourself, you can heal by developing self-soothing techniques, communicating transparently about your fears and needs with your partner, and seeking therapy to address underlying worries.

Dismissive Avoidant Attachment

'I don't like getting too close to people. Emotions make me uncomfortable, and I prefer to handle things on my own.'

This style might develop if you had emotionally distant or dismissive parents. Dismissive avoidant attachment looks like:

- Avoiding intimacy and emotional closeness.
- Preferring independence and self-reliance.
- Feeling uncomfortable with vulnerability.
- Feeling suffocated in relationships and unwilling to make a commitment.
- Concealing or failing to express your caring thoughts and feelings.

If you have a dismissive avoidant attachment style, relating comfortably to others as adults requires effort and conscious work around emotional communication and intimacy. You might find it helpful to unpack formative relationship patterns with a therapist.

Fearful (Disorganized) Avoidant Attachment

'I want to be close to someone, but I'm also scared they'll hurt me. I can be hot and cold in relationships.'

This dynamic typically results from inconsistent caregiving and early trauma. It looks like:

- Feeling profound conflict about intimacy. You simultaneously crave and fear close emotional bonds.

- Swinging between guarding yourself against anticipated rejection and desperately seeking connection when you're feeling lonely.

- Avoiding relationships to minimize your chances of getting hurt, even though you might crave affection and love.

If these look or sound familiar to you, professional counselling can help you to address the past and build your capacity for trust and regulation in present relationships.

* * *

Attachment styles affect all of our relationships, not just romantic ones. Understanding them can be helpful when it comes to building more supportive relationships.

Although we can never completely understand another person, or be in control of our own responses to emotional triggers, we can gain some awareness of where those reactions come from and be more compassionate towards ourselves and the other person.

I mention compassion because it's an essential part of any relationship. If you look solely at someone's reaction to a situation, a lot of misunderstanding can follow. You might misinterpret their behaviour, think they are deliberately trying to hurt you or don't love you enough. By having some compassion, you will see them through a totally different lens and have a much better chance of working things out as a team.

Many of us have a mixture of attachment styles, with one more dominant than the other – and we can also show different attachment styles in different kinds of relationships, which continue to change throughout our lifetime. Although we develop these attachment styles as babies, it doesn't mean we are incapable of changing them. If you'd like to learn more, there's a great book on the subject by Amir Levine and Rachel Heller called *Attached*.

When attachment styles meet

A person with an anxious attachment style can find themselves in an endless loop with someone with an avoidant style. As the avoidant person pulls away to protect their independence and freedom, the anxious person pushes for more closeness, which creates further distance.

This is common in all relationships, and I would propose that to some degree this is normal human behaviour. Nevertheless, as attachment styles are patterns of behaviours, this dynamic can continue unless a conscious effort is made to heal the wounds creating them.

Here are how other pairings might play out:

Secure–Secure

When two individuals with secure attachment styles come together, they have the capacity to create a strong, healthy and supportive relationship. They communicate openly, trust each other, and provide emotional support without hesitation. Conflict resolution is generally effective, and it can help couples to navigate challenges together with empathy and understanding.

Anxious–Anxious

In a relationship between two anxious individuals, there may be intense emotional connection and a strong desire for reassurance and closeness. However, both partners might also struggle with insecurity and occasional jealousy. It can be a loving relationship, but they may need to work on managing their anxiety-related issues to maintain harmony.

Avoidant–Avoidant

When two avoidant individuals are in a relationship, they prioritize independence and personal space over emotional intimacy. They may maintain a certain emotional distance from each other, leading to a lack of deep connection. These relationships can be stable but might lack emotional depth.

Secure–Anxious

A partnership between a secure and an anxious individual can be beneficial, with the secure partner providing reassurance and understanding to meet the anxious partner's needs for validation and closeness. This balance can lead to a loving and supportive relationship.

Secure–Avoidant

In this combination, the secure partner may help the avoidant partner become more comfortable with emotional intimacy over time. The secure partner's ability to provide reassurance while respecting the avoidant partner's need for space can lead to a well-balanced relationship.

Determining your predominant attachment style (with a therapist's help or an online test) allows you to understand and start improving your relationship reactions. While professional support can unravel the roots behind your patterns, self-insight is the first step.

We all crave intimate connections, but we may struggle depending on our attachments. Remember, these are coping behaviours shaped by your experiences, not core personality traits. With an empathetic partner and personal effort, needs can be met and attachments can shift from fearful to secure.

This requires recognizing vulnerabilities and releasing patterns that are no longer serving you. Progress takes self-compassion and diligence, and requires you to refuse relationships that enable old wounds. If someone is unable to support your needs, it could point to a poor match – or a partner unable to grow at present. Seek those who help you safely transition into secure functioning.

Honour your emotional needs instead of repressing them to keep the peace. Openness allows your partner to fully know and accept you too. When you embrace yourself, insecurities transform into intimate security.

Maybe people aren't leaving you.

Maybe the Universe is leaving room in your life for people who appreciate and reciprocate the love you share.

PART THREE

Cultivating Healthy Bonds

Your partner is your mirror

Turn your magnifying glass into a mirror.
When you begin to analyze and focus on
other people's flaws, stop for a moment,
and see what it reveals about you.

A romantic partner can be a mirror showing you your spiritual reflection. They reflect back traits you may struggle to see clearly in yourself. Through this mirroring, your loved one offers you tremendous potential for growth and self-discovery, if you have the courage to look.

At times the image can seem harsh, even ugly. When your partner reflects behaviours you don't accept within yourself, it hurts. But it's the emotional lesson that's often the true challenge, not the person or circumstance delivering it.

Either way, we can use all our relationships in this world – romantic or otherwise – to know love.

Your partner can help uncover deeper capacities for patience, forgiveness and compassion within you if you approach challenges with an open heart. Much of what they can show you is really an unlearning.

Here's an example. Let's say you have a tendency to totally shut down when fights get heated. Like a turtle retreating into its shell, you get stoney-faced and dead silent. At first, this can look pretty dramatic to your partner, who is left freaking out even more. They get super frustrated and put their hands up, in a gesture of 'Please say something instead of just bailing'.

And that reaction ends up being a harsh but helpful mirror reflecting this emotional shut-down habit back at you. You get to see for yourself how the silent treatment actually hurts the people you care about and hinders your connection. Not only is it an important 'aha' moment, it is also an opportunity to work through why you avoid vulnerability like this, so you can unlearn a harmful old habit.

Or your partner's attentiveness in reminding you of appointments, despite your forgetfulness, could demonstrate unconditional support. Receiving such care when you least deserve it might soften hardness within, helping you extend more grace towards your own flaws.

Your partner can mirror back both shadow and light within you, if you seek the lesson rather than assigning blame. With openness, we help each other rise higher.

Remember the ball image we talked about? At the centre, we're all one. The expressions of love on the outside of the ball may be limited and temporary, but they all connect back to the centre. In fact, the centre of the ball and the outside of the ball are always one thing, for they cannot exist without each other.

The trouble comes when we don't know how to properly connect those two things. Our focus is on the other person, instead of the heart.

We see their limits, their faults and imperfections, as well as our own, instead of unique expressions of one perfect love.

We think our differences are hassles, rather than complementary facets of one and the same diamond.

We think that spiritual love and romantic love belong in different boxes. To mix them is unthinkable.

Even more problematic, we think of ourselves as small, lonely, broken and dented little things, instead of expressions of the one vast Universe.

Facing your unmet needs

As we've learned, how you connect with yourself and the world around you is no accident. Your entire perception of relationships is shaped by your early life experiences.

No one embarks on a relationship with a clean slate – we all have a past, which forms a large part of how we think today. How we were brought up, childhood memories, cultural beliefs, personal relationship experiences, the job we do – our mind is absolutely stuffed with preconceptions.

We all come with some type of baggage,
whether it's trauma or unresolved pain. A precious
relationship is one with someone who wants to
unpack the baggage with you. With a lighter load
you make more space for authentic love.

Since it's impossible to enter a relationship without some emotional baggage, a healthy connection with someone becomes a beautiful place to unpack it – if you have the right tools and support. Love has the capacity to bring light to the dark corridors of any heart. For many, the light of true love is bright enough to expose beliefs, habits, mindsets and behaviours that directly impact the quality of connections.

So many of us want someone who is already healed. But life is constantly handing us circumstances to heal through and grow through. The process never stops.

It can be disheartening to find the right person only to discover you may not be prepared to foster a healthy relationship with them, like laying out the soil for a garden and realizing you have no seeds to plant into it. Relationships magnify the missing pieces of our emotional puzzle, pieces a partner cannot fit for us. After all, they have their own jigsaw to solve.

While a partner may see and experience the vast landscape of your personality, they get the bad with the good. They see traits that only emerge within a romantic dynamic. Along with the snorting laughter, questionable taste in music and terrible jokes, they'll be the witness of your deepest wounding. They will see how remnants of your caregivers' patterns show up in conflict. You may even surprise yourself with the way unconscious conditioning takes the driver's seat.

Do you try to control every outcome or conversation? Often, underneath this need to control is a feeling of insecurity when things get unpredictable. Sudden changes may echo episodes of instability or chaos in your past. For example, constantly moving homes as a child or having unreliable caregivers can breed persistent feelings of insecurity and lack of control. Later in life, this can manifest as trying to tightly orchestrate situations and relationships to compensate for that early uncertainty.

Do you tend to behave like a people-pleaser? This habit often comes from our childhood. Love gets presented to us as something that we have to earn. It gets connected to the anxious need to seek approval from others. For instance, you only felt loved if you got high marks in an exam. Love wasn't given freely; instead, you had to perform to get it. As an adult now, you echo that pattern by trying to please people in order to be accepted and validated. You have internalized that pattern, and it's hard to break.

Do you find yourself over-explaining your opinions and thoughts? This tendency can originate from childhood environments where you had your reality shut down and your feelings dismissed. Perhaps you continue to repeat points to justify your case, or use more words and details than necessary when explaining what you mean. Or maybe you find yourself pursuing a lost cause when someone is clearly choosing to misunderstand you. You feel that they must believe you, agree with you and validate your truth to feel a sense of security. I've often seen this play out with the youngest sibling, where their views might have been disregarded or misinterpreted because they were seen as naive. Later, in life partnerships, an over-explaining habit can strain communication – though its core aim is for understanding.

In intimate bonds, our coping strategies and traumas surface. What we avoid facing alone now stands glaringly before us. Rather than shame the parts of you that are still hurting, meet their presence with curiosity and care. Ask what positive intention or past requirement shaped each habit. Bring awareness and understanding to the wounded inner child with the mature care and wisdom of our healthy adult self. Nurturing them as if we are now the good, attuned parent that perhaps wasn't present early on.

When we start to spot the needs that weren't met for us in our childhood, we can begin to meet them now, as adults. Giving ourselves the missing care lets these inner child parts mature and develop in healthier ways, transforming old wounds and beliefs.

Relationships can help us heal old wounds – if we let them. If you're ready to courageously face those uncomfortable parts of yourself, your partner can be your spiritual guide.

What beliefs have shaped the way you love?

Like soft cookie dough, you are born with a tender and innate capacity to experience, desire and share the sweetest kind of love. But undesirable cookie-cutter experiences can reshape the way you mould your relationships. It isn't until learned patterns melt away that we can redefine how we experience love.

Use these prompts to explore potholes in your perception of the world, the way you love and how you connect with others. Unfold the values that have shaped your every relationship.

Make room inside your heart and create space around your thoughts and feelings. Don't sink into the emotional experience – just pay attention to what it's taught you. We're trying to re-learn from a place of loving awareness.

1. What cultural, societal and parental influences were you raised on?

Example: 'I was raised with a blend of traditional Indian and British cultural values as the daughter of immigrant Hindu parents trying to preserve their heritage. There were strong community and religious influences from our temple and Indian social circle. My parents emphasized academic achievement as vital and insisted on no relationships until I had finished studying.'

2. What beliefs, traditions, customs or norms were imposed on you?

Example: 'There were expectations around duty to family, future career choices deemed "respectable", preserving customs around holidays/weddings, criteria for a suitable husband, gender roles in marriage and principles about sexuality, dating and behaviour. I internalized norms valuing modesty, indirect communication, avoiding confrontation/setting boundaries with elders and superiors.'

3. How many of these conditions are you still living by?

Example: 'I still largely adhere to upholding family reputation, career ambition in a stable field and emotional restraint in relationships. However, I've adopted more egalitarian views on gender, sexuality and self-expression from peers. I feel tension balancing traditional expectations at home with liberal social values.'

4. Who most impacted how you determine what is right or wrong, good or bad for you? What were some of these ideas?

Example: 'My parents and relatives most shaped my right/ wrong perspectives – their approval meant everything.

Disappointing family was the "worst" behaviour. I learned high ethical standards but also tendencies like guilt, doubt about acting independently and speaking directly about problems.'

5. If your caregivers told you what is right or wrong, who told them and how was that confirmed?

Example: 'My caregivers learned principles about duty, family hierarchy and gender propriety from previous generations and through Hindu/Indian community norms. In the name of preserving virtue – as defined by their heritage – these perspectives went unchallenged. If we swayed from tradition, aunts and uncles slammed that shut quick. Their heavy disapproval pressured us to conform even more.'

6. How do these conditions seem to come up in your personal relationships?

Example: 'I notice a tendency to want to control my partner. Having caregivers and family who expected a lot from me has made me hypercritical of my spouse's decisions.'

We are all creatures of our environment, but you can, and should, be able to live by the personal value system that feels right for you, whether that goes against the current norms or not.

If you value honesty in a relationship, make room for it by opening up to your own truths.

If you want to experience compassion, you need to be compassionate with yourself.

By overcoming habitual thought patterns, you can create space for spontaneity, flexibility, objectivity, independence – all things that build beautiful relationships.

When you remove fear, you are free to enjoy life more.

It is possible to become a vibrational match to the relationship you desire. Once you delve into your depths and realize the capacity you have to love yourself, without the need for your partner to fill a void, you can attract someone who is coming from the same level of awareness. Your relationship will be about thriving together, not a survival course.

Vulnerability lets you stand in your power

When you have two people willing to be vulnerable,
a magical safety between you occurs. With no words,
you are communicating with one another,
'You are safe here. I am safe here.
Let's be here together. Completely.'

Imagine someone gets hold of your personal journal and broadcasts your innermost thoughts and feelings to the world. From secrets to hidden desires, you are entirely exposed. This may seem dramatic, but when you decide to open up to someone new, the emotional response in your body can be just as intense.

From the moment we're born, we're encouraged to protect ourselves. A child must have its food chopped up into tiny bits, a kid must wear a flotation ring in the pool, a teen must be guided on how to handle peer pressure and set healthy boundaries. We are raised to do everything we can to be cautious and to stay out of harm's way.

But there comes a point when the instinct to protect ourselves can stop us from growing. Because we'll only really connect with another person if we allow ourselves to be vulnerable.

Most of us have a tremendous fear around deep emotions, and we will do whatever it takes to protect ourselves from being shamed, hurt, ridiculed or taken advantage of.

It might not be obvious that you're uncomfortable with being vulnerable, or with creating emotional intimacy. Guard yourself long enough, it just becomes second nature. Struggling with vulnerability can look like down-playing your feelings or experiences.

Have you shared a painful part of your past only to follow it with 'but it's no big deal'? Or, on the contrary, when someone else begins to open up, do you find yourself distancing at the sight of their vulnerability? Or perhaps even making a joke or saying something funny to deflect from the seriousness? Much of this stems from fear. The fear of being seen because it can lead to rejection, or opening up because it forces you to feel emotions you've been avoiding.

But distancing from vulnerability is a sure way to limit connections. Vulnerability invites something called reciprocal self-disclosure, which means the mutual sharing of personal information, thoughts or feelings between individuals in a conversation or relationship. When people say they feel close to someone, this is what they usually mean; they've built trust, fostered intimacy and strengthened their connection by creating a sense of shared understanding and a deeper level of communication.

It takes humility, compassion and grace to open up and trust. These are all roadways to the centre of our being, the love that accepts all things. To shut the door tightly is to close the door to the centre – to the connection with that love.

Vulnerability isn't just about exposing your weaknesses

To be vulnerable is to know yourself, accept yourself and be at peace with what you can and cannot offer someone. It's a bold demonstration of self-acceptance and an invitation for others to do the same.

When you meet and connect with someone new, the dynamic of your life changes. You're pushed to consider new ways of being – ways you might not be prepared for. Rejecting these new options because you are too shut down is going to prevent you from forming a deeper connection with your partner.

Connection is made through authentic emotional expression.

When you have two people willing to be vulnerable, you make space for an extraordinary safety between you to develop.

Vulnerability is the key to intimacy and healing. It's the secret to selflessness and a deeper love.

Bear in mind that vulnerability also needs boundaries: it's not about oversharing and leaving yourself totally exposed. You don't need to hand over the keys to your entire house of suppressed feelings, shameful experiences and unedited internal struggles. Neither is it the same as an emotional outburst. The goal is not to burden people with your feelings and share your entire life story, but to share openly in a safe space.

In order for anyone to open up, they need a level of trust that a worthy partner has demonstrated consistently. Nobody should throw themselves recklessly into an emotional situation if the other person hasn't proved that they will be supportive and caring. That would only lead to distrust and a failure to genuinely connect.

But we should be prepared to take that leap of faith when we find someone who maybe, just maybe, can enrich our lives. Even if letting the walls down doesn't come naturally, it's worth it. If a relationship doesn't last, at least you can say you showed up. You didn't present only a portion of who you are.

Dare to love

We're more vulnerable with our bodies than our emotions these days. We're more comfortable with getting physically intimate with strangers than emotionally intimate with loved ones. Satisfying sexual urges not only feels rewarding, it also provides a fleeting hit of pseudo-connection without having to face the discomfort of laying ourselves emotionally bare. To unmask insecurities and reveal hidden dreams feels far more exposing than showing skin.

You don't have to learn how to be vulnerable. Remember that we were born fragile and completely dependent on others. We are born vulnerable.

Nevertheless, you might need to practise communicating from a place of vulnerability. Be kind with yourself as you move forward with courage. You can't get closer to someone if you keep building a brick wall between you. Even if they try to scale it a few times, they'll eventually get fed up and walk away.

It's OK to let them know that you feel vulnerable. Allow them to be vulnerable, too, and make them feel safe when they are. By discussing your fears and anxieties, you are also inviting them to talk about themselves, which helps to foster greater intimacy and invites them to be an active participant in the experience by offering you comfort or reassurance. They may even share that this level of intimacy is new for them – what a unique chance to explore a new path together.

When you feel supported and cared for, there is nothing stopping you expressing all that you think and feel. Your partner will appreciate it and feel able to do the same.

Practices that cultivate vulnerability

- Ease into self-expression. Start with things you're comfortable sharing and slowly progress into more complex subjects. They can be as small as a guilty pleasure when it comes to taste in music – like admitting you're secretly a Swiftie (a hardcore Taylor Swift fan).

- Be honest about going into vulnerability so they know that you're working through some internal limitations.

- Affirm to them and yourself that they make you feel comfortable enough to open up. You're sharing with them because there's a level of trust that has been established.

- Remember how important and valuable vulnerability is for the growth and deepening of the connection. Confirm that the other person feels the same.

- Choose a setting that feels safe and conducive to emotional intimacy. Make sure you don't feel rushed, restricted or confined by the environment. A busy bar might not be the ideal location for this sort of discussion.

- Be compassionate and gentle with yourself and others. Don't worry about sounding awkward or fumbling your words. The key is just getting them out.

- Don't force yourself to be vulnerable. The experience shouldn't be entirely uncomfortable. It must be supported by some level of emotional safety.

Vulnerability will do more than just enrich your relationships, it increases your empathy, enhances communication skills, strengthens self-trust, helps overcome ego-driven stories and infuses your life with authenticity.

Our ego is like a protective shield, always on the lookout for threats. While it's helpful, it can make it hard to open up to love. When the ego is in control, we struggle to connect with our true selves and feel love. Being vulnerable helps break down these barriers and allows us to experience love more freely.

Trust starts with you

'The best way to find out if you can trust somebody is to trust them.'
Ernest Hemingway

Vulnerability is just one of many gateways to getting to know ourselves and others. In the early stages of dating someone, we're learning about a potential partner's patterns and behaviours. The excitement of a new relationship is a real high, and it is also a time when you feel incredibly vulnerable. You like someone and hope that they like you too, but the thing between you is still new and delicate.

The what-ifs loom large. Can I trust them? Will I get hurt again?

You could let fear win and guard your heart like a gated house. Or you can bravely lean into the beauty and uncertainty of human connection. This takes trust – in yourself, in them, in the process. Easier said than done, I know.

We can't control others. But we can model healthy behaviours ourselves to set the tone. That's why I say that trust starts with you. Having faith in your judgement won't guarantee a partner's honesty, but it helps you stand firmly in your worth when navigating relationships.

Think of self-trust as the harness securing you on this crazy ride. By believing in your ability to handle twists and turns, you can enjoy the thrills – shared dreams, laughter, spicy takeaways at midnight. And if things get bumpy, your sense of inner strength helps you stay grounded and clear-headed.

Grounding your decisions in the faith you have in yourself means you'll be less likely to be taken advantage of, or experience unhealthy levels of jealousy, and you will be more capable of contributing to a healthy dynamic.

Here are a few ways you can lead with trust in a relationship:

- Be consistent. Your actions match your words. The integrity of your word is crucial in a connection. It's critical your partner can trust what you tell them.

- Be honest with yourself. This empowers you to take accountability for behaviours that impact your relationships. When you can get real about the role you play in conflicts, healing and addressing issues becomes more straightforward.

- Be discerning. In the early stages of a connection, self-trust will help you determine whether to stay or go. You'll be discerning with your time, energy and emotions.

- Be clear about your needs. This is essential to feeling seen and supported. Self-trust is a pillar for someone who values their personal needs.

Cultivating self-trust

You might be wondering how you can build self-trust. It circles back to getting to know yourself and loving yourself on deeper levels. Here are some ideas that might help:

- Understand your needs, values, strengths and weaknesses through self-reflection. This will build confidence to act on your own wisdom.

- Practise self-validation rather than seeking external approval. Replace self-doubting inner voices with compassionate self-acknowledgement so you no longer second-guess yourself.

- Keep daily promises to yourself. Start small; for example, begin with basic self-care routines like keeping up with your daily schedule, getting enough sleep or taking reflective walks. Knowing that you can honour your commitments helps you build towards maintaining bigger life goals.

- Heal past hurts (like betrayal) to improve your decision-making ability and help you to notice warning signs. Healing brings clarity and reconnects you to your inner GPS, your intuition, without being clouded by pain disguised as fear.

- Celebrate and appreciate yourself for progress made and personal strengths, rather than focusing only on weaknesses and failures. Self-trust has very much to do with acknowledging your victories and believing in your abilities.

Honesty increases intimacy

Without respectful honesty, there is no trust; without trust, there is no safety; without safety, there is no intimacy; and without intimacy, there is no connection.

Honesty and trust are two sides of the same coin. Being honest with your partner allows them to get to know you and increases intimacy.

It's common (and often healthy) to want to put your best foot forward. We tend to want to present ourselves as all put-together – hiding the scars, covering up the shame and tucking away the skeletons.

But there's only so much you can hide from a relationship. Eventually, the mask will slip. And your partner will finally see the totality of you. Your completeness. If they're standing in a space of unconditional love, it will make them more interested in you.

When you wear the mask for too long, when your relationship feels more like a performance than an authentically lived experience, you are forfeiting trust and closeness.

Dishonesty can begin with little things – like hiding how much money you've spent, for example, or lying about the last two drinks you had on your night out with friends – until it becomes a habit you adopt to avoid arguments.

When you lack self-trust, you might reproduce the following unhealthy patterns:

- Your partner is honest but you still disbelieve what they say, or assume the worst.
- You question their motives and intentions, making intimacy impossible.
- You self-sabotage the relationship now rather than risk disappointment later.
- You are plagued by feelings of regret, guilt, shame and bitterness.

Just because someone let you down in the past, it doesn't mean the same thing will happen in the future. Once you've developed trust in your own judgement and value, it is possible to build up trust slowly in your next relationship.

It's all about balance here – when trust is broken, don't rush into something new too quickly. Stay open to meeting someone that you will be happy to have in your life. Resist the desire to control the situation.

It's OK to talk about your trust issues when you start seeing someone new – although you don't need to go into every detail just yet. Explain that you had a bad experience and are trying to work through it, allowing your new partner to understand where you are coming from.

Communicate in a calm, authentic way and be vulnerable. You can ask your partner their opinion, or if they have had a similar experience.

What makes fulfilling relationships

Vulnerability, trust and honesty are in the toolkit that every fulfilling connection needs. If we're going to experience something real, we have to be willing to be real. Despite how uncomfortable and revealing the process may seem, despite how risky and vulnerable it gets, you keep going.

Keeping it real saves you so much time and energy.
You discover who appreciates you as you are, who else
is being themselves, and you free yourself from the
burden of maintaining a fake connection that doesn't
align with your deepest beliefs and values.

Keep trusting that this is what you want – someone who knows, sees and loves you for who you are. Perfectly imperfect. Lead your relationships with truth. Seek raw emotional experiences. You will find more love the deeper you go into the well.

A trusting relationship is based on a deep inner trust of life. When we realize, in a deep and authentic way, that life is not something we have to conquer, master and plan, that it is something to experience and explore instead, then we can let go and begin to trust it. Inwardly, this releases a great deal of tension. It frees up wellsprings of energy, which you can share with your loved one.

Setting boundaries is an act of love

*You can be a loving person who respects people's
needs and still set boundaries that protect yours.*

It's easy to get so caught up in a new relationship that everything
else falls away.

But getting closer to your new partner shouldn't mean forsaking
your beliefs, interests, hobbies, friends, or anything else. It's
possible to form a caring, fulfilling relationship without letting go
of who you are – even if many of us find this hard to do.

Protecting your boundaries in any relationship is crucial if you
want to retain your sense of identity. It's easy to fall into the
pattern of becoming 'one' with the other and losing yourself on
the way. In all relationships, boundaries help us to stay true to
ourselves while respecting the other person.

Exploring the depths of yourself is a crucial part of your spiritual
journey. Relationships can reflect this process, helping you let go
of harmful ego identities. However, it's important not to replace

them with another false identity – one that's merged with someone else's. You might be connected via the same source, but you are still two individuals on separate journeys.

Types of boundaries to set in a relationship

Before setting boundaries, consider what you need in a relationship to retain your autonomy, and to feel respected and at peace.

Get clear on your non-negotiable boundaries. List them out. These are the lines others cannot cross if you are to have an intimate, healthy relationship with them. It might be useful to reflect on any unhealthy patterns in your relationship that you want to change – for example, your partner always shouting over you when you have a difference of opinion.

Next, reconnect to your inherent self-worth. Our value exists intrinsically, it is not defined by others. Let this truth sink in deeply.

When we don't know our worth, it's easy for a critical partner to make us shrink back or lash out at them. But when we stand confident in our values, we can lovingly assert boundaries from a grounded place.

Once you know your needs, limits and intrinsic worth, you can address the relationship compassionately. Boundaries should be set in a calm and private moment – not mid-argument.

Nevertheless, sometimes boundaries must be asserted during heated moments where you are being disrespected. It is important to make sure you take a few deep breaths to calm your nervous system before you relay your limits.

Here are the types of boundaries you might set.

Communication boundaries

Establish topics, tone and language that isn't invited into your conversations, especially during moments of conflict or disagreements.

Examples:

'I'm not ready to discuss this subject right now. If you bring it up, I'm not having this conversation anymore.'

'Whoa, when you start yelling like that, I don't feel heard or safe, to be honest. If you keep getting louder, I'll have to pause this talk until we both chill out a bit emotionally.'

Physical boundaries

Define your comfort levels when it comes to touch, physical affection and intimacy. Establish the importance of consent and having regular conversations about who is comfortable with what.

Examples:

'As much as I love kissing you, I prefer not to do it in public. Let's save that level of intimacy for when we're in a private space.'

'All the touching lately is feeling like a bit much for me right now. Let's take it down a notch with the physical stuff until I'm ready.'

Emotional boundaries

Be clear about emotional needs, expectations and limits.

Examples:

'I need some time to myself to recharge after work. Let's set aside an hour in the evenings just for self-care where we do our own thing.'

'I think we've got to check in about what we both want and need here. What's working for you, what's not working? I'll share my piece too and hopefully we can get on the same page.'

Remember that boundaries are a form of self-care. They don't make you less compassionate but help you keep your relationships healthy without suffocating yourself.

The right people won't feel threatened by your boundaries and will respect you for standing your ground. It goes without saying that boundaries aren't meant to be used to hide damaging secrets. This would just be manipulation and flat-out deceit.

Airing your feelings out in the open is honest and healthy. Bottling them up and expecting the other person to guess your feelings leads to misunderstandings.

Consider where your boundaries are coming from

If you've put the feelings and needs of others before your own too many times, healthy boundaries bring such a relief. Boundaries teach you to accurately measure how much energy you can give before requiring a recharge session.

Boundaries also prevent resentment towards people you care about. By creating a healthy dynamic that allows you to honour your needs, you can show up happily and authentically to your connections.

But sometimes, boundaries can go too far.

By assuming that everyone is going to ruin your peace and drain you, you may pre-emptively enforce a boundary. The perceived threat could actually be a fear of being vulnerable.

By finding internal safety and a sense of awareness, vulnerability won't be so intimidating and you'll be able to set boundaries from a place of inner security rather than defensiveness. That sense of balance comes when you are connected to the boundless power source at the centre of our being. In that connection, your personal energy is resolved and recharged. You recognize people have to fuel themselves and you're not responsible for fixing everyone's problems or giving them what they want, you only need to maintain your own connection to the centre of your being. This transforms your sense of duty, which is often draining, into sharing and connecting, which feels energizing.

It's called a boundary because it's the line where you and another person meet. It's the point where limits misalign, and an understanding must be defined.

Yet, too many boundaries posed too soon can come off as an attempt to control a situation instead of extending trust in others and inviting them to express themselves. Throwing up a caution sign before you need to could push good people away.

The hows of healthy boundaries

Use this checklist to help you understand and set boundaries that allow love to grow instead of pushing it out.

Boundaries that help love grow:

- Emerge from a place of self-love and personal well-being.
- Protect the connection between you and your partner.
- Encourage you and your partner to have individual autonomy within the relationship.
- Support your personal and relational growth.
- Come about naturally as a response to an event.

Boundaries that push love out:

- Include rigid rules designed to control or manipulate.

- Arise from fear, leading to insecurity and mistrust.

- Go against, or get in the way of, the values and beliefs of another person.

- Impose rules without thinking about what the other person needs or wants.

- Suppress individual expression and growth.

If you're flexible with your boundaries, people will be flexible with how they treat you.

Every relationship
needs expectations to thrive

You're not asking for too much when you seek someone who considers how their actions, words and lack of communication impact you. It's OK to wait for someone who's willing to show up daily to sustain the connection. You deserve to be cared for.

Picture the scene: you're on a first date, you're having a fun, flirty time. Out of nowhere, your date pulls out their phone and hits you with . . . a checklist.

It sounds extreme, but it's more common than you might realize. Some buddies of mine once quoted things their dates read out loud from their notes app. While some expectations seemed reasonable – like kindness and a healthy work ethic – there were others that seemed overwhelming, strange and unrealistic. 'Mustn't let others merge in their lane during traffic because it shows a sign of weakness.' Wait, what?!

The impersonal nature of the list of expectations can make you feel like you're at a job interview and not on a first date.

Relationship expectations are personal beliefs about what a relationship should look like. They exist so we can fulfil our desires or to help us avoid pain. We develop some of these expectations after previous partners failed to meet them.

But too many expectations suffocate the relationship before it has a chance to form. Your checklist might be so comprehensive that no human can measure up to it.

Fewer expectations in a relationship give more opportunities for unconditional love to arise. They encourage full acceptance of the human in front of you.

With fewer expectations, you stop outsourcing so many of your emotional needs to another – needs you are capable of meeting for yourself. This helps avoid a purely transactional relationship.

Lists of 'dos' and 'don'ts' may reveal your fundamental mistrust in the process of life. When you are secure in your own connection to the love that lives at the centre of your being, and trust that it will bring you what you most want, it's much easier to give a potential partner the benefit of the doubt.

Nevertheless, it's good to know what you want. We need some expectations to sustain a healthy relationship, because, as mentioned before, human beings have limits. That's why it's helpful to look at expectations as healthy and unhealthy.

Healthy relationship expectations include:

- My partner will consider how their behaviour affects me.
- My partner will be affectionate physically and verbally.
- There will be a balance of quality time and alone time within the relationship.
- My partner will be interested in who I am, the things I care about and my major life choices.
- My partner offers comfort, compassion and care when I am sad or hurting.
- My partner is faithful once we agree to be exclusive.
- It is safe to disagree with my partner without fear of ridicule.
- My partner will encourage what is best for me.

Unhealthy relationship expectations include:

- My partner will put me above everyone and everything.
- My partner will make me happy.
- My partner will bend to my will.
- My partner will always align with me mentally, emotionally and spiritually.

- We will never fight or disagree.
- My partner will never complain about me or the relationship.
- I own my partner's body and they own mine.

Expectations and reality

There will be times when people let you down. When things don't go your way, you may feel disappointed and hurt. We're always expecting the world to adjust to and meet our needs.

But we can't control other people's actions, only our own. How people act is merely a manifestation of their inner world.

Our expectations can direct us towards changes we need to make within – for example, a craving for somebody's presence might reveal a void that's shouting out for our attention.

It's impractical to drop all of our expectations because they often help us become aware of what we deserve. Instead:

- Realize that expectations can hinder inner peace.
- Discover how they might affect you on your inner healing journey.
- Identify shifts you need to make in your relationships.

Reducing expectations and not taking things personally are liberating acts. One way I try to do this is to assume the best in others

– by encouraging compassion, you can break the connection to the outcome you craved. Allow life to unfold as it will, from the centre of love, and you'll usually be delighted by the surprise, even if it isn't what you thought you wanted.

As morbid as this sounds, if a loved one disappoints me, I tell myself that it could be the last time I ever see or speak to them. This inspires gratitude and allows me to enjoy their presence, rather than focusing on what expectations of mine they aren't fulfilling. Also, remember that no one's flawless, including yourself. People don't always get it right. Life would be quite dull if everything was always perfect, and seen from this perspective, in a sense, everything is perfectly imperfect.

Gratitude closes the distance between expectation and reality, which ultimately reduces the amount of suffering we experience in the present moment.

Cultivating gratitude is a powerful antidote if disappointment arises from unmet expectations. Gratitude affirms that what we have in our life is worthy of being thankful for despite expectations. Suffering subsides when you're in a state of genuine appreciation.

It hurts when people don't do for you what you'd do for them in a heartbeat. Nevertheless, releasing expectations is the surest way to stop people from having the power to hurt you. Just know your worth – so you can identify who's worthy of your time and energy.

Love speaks many languages

Someone can speak your love language for a moment, but that doesn't mean they belong in your life forever.

When author Gary Chapman defined the 'five love languages' in his 1992 book of the same name, he described the five different ways people give and receive love, based loosely on attachment styles. They are: words of affirmation (compliments), quality time, the giving of gifts, acts of service and physical touch.

In recent years, this framework has exploded into the popular consciousness, and become part of our shared discourse. You've probably seen it on social media and people's dating profiles: 'My primary love language is words of affirmation.'

But love languages existed long before Gary Chapman packaged them into catchy categories of how we express ourselves.

They were just things we did for each other. They were ways that we expressed love from the centre of our being and made it tangible for those we cared about.

And though this model offers intriguing insights, stick to it too closely and it may well limit how you experience love and connect with others.

Love languages evolve

At one stage of your life, you might have valued physical touch above other means of connection. But later on, you might have discovered that quality time has a greater impact on your quality of intimacy.

Love languages change, and we shouldn't feel limited to one or two.

The idea that our love languages should be fixed and determined – and that they need to be compatible with our partner's – is like limiting ourselves to a fixed set of words in the English language. By selecting just a few phrases, you're stopping yourself from engaging in and experiencing an expansive conversation. It can destroy spontaneity and the flow of the moment. You might end up living in the theory, instead of the real present moment.

Similarly, identifying the 'best' ways to perceive love only limits your capacity to give and receive it.

When we open our hearts and minds to the energy of love, it becomes apparent that it shows up for us in a million different ways.

Love isn't transactional

Taken to an extreme, the love languages framework might lead you to start tracking how often your partner expresses love in your preferred language, and keeping score. That's transactional, and not from the heart.

'I feel loved when you offer words of affirmation.'

If your partner had roses delivered to you instead of telling you how proud they are of you, would you disregard the gesture? Would you find yourself waiting for their spoken or written words instead?

When we keep tabs on what *isn't* done for us, it's easy to overlook what has been done for us – all the ways love was expressed in other moments.

Love languages can become destructive categories by which we track our partner's rights and wrongs and unconsciously calculate whether we're loved or not.

This is a complete disservice to relationships and a poor substitute for demonstrating genuine feelings.

Love languages can hold you back

Sometimes our selected love language teaches our partners, friends and family to give us what we want, but not what we need.

Your preferred love languages could stem from wounding. If a life of lack has kept you in survival mode, you may seek physical demonstrations of love, like gifts.

From years of neglect, your mind has learned to interpret someone taking care of your basic monetary needs as an act of love – when consistency, safety and stability within a relationship would be more suitable for your spirit. Gifts would then just become generous expressions, but not how you feel most loved.

Never allow your love language to overshadow harmful behaviour. If your love language ever fell into the wrong hands, it could be used to manipulate you into accepting unacceptable treatment.

For example, Josh's primary love language is quality time. He feels most cherished when his partner listens attentively, without distractions.

His new boyfriend, Jacob, seemed perfect at first – doting on him with long phone calls and weekend getaways. Josh felt he really 'got' him.

But after a few blissful months, Jacob's verbal abuse began. Any slight frustration provoked nasty outbursts towards Josh. After just six months together, he hardly recognized himself or the relationship.

Yet whenever Jacob sensed Josh pulling away after an explosive fight, he would bombard him with gifts and undivided attention. Candle-lit dinners, inside jokes whispered breathlessly, gazing soulfully into his eyes again.

Josh's yearning for Jacob's sweet attentiveness always got him hooked back in. But the blow-ups inevitably resumed . . . and intensified. Jewellery to apologize for a split lip; a holiday to soothe the pain of the bruises.

Josh's top love language made him vulnerable to manipulation. Jacob exploited his craving for quality time to keep Josh bonded through the violence and degradation.

Expand your love vocabulary

Beyond touch, gifts, words of affirmation, quality time and acts of service, here are a few other love languages to help expand your relationship vocabulary.

Patience. Forgiveness. Listening. Awareness. Friendship. Accountability. Teamwork. Shared values and beliefs. Compassion. Authentic communication. Reassurance. Personal and relationship growth. Future planning. Flirting. Shared memes. Comfortable silences.

The ways in which we share and receive love can't be reduced into just five categories. So don't attempt to categorize love.

It's the nature of the ego-mind to want to minimize big emotions and experiences so that we can better define, understand and control them, but the heart knows better. The very nature of love is that it can't be completely defined. A single act cannot embody the entire essence of love.

Love doesn't need to shout, or brag or put on a show. It is the quiet voice in the heart.

My suggestion? Instead of finding ways to define love and to speak its language, find more ways to become aware of it. Notice it in the simple, undefined, quiet and limitless nature with which it unveils itself.

Communicating with care
brings us closer

A wedding, a baby, a holiday, a new house, a move abroad – none of these will fix the problems in a relationship. You can only heal a relationship from the inside out, with honesty, vulnerability and a mutual desire to do the work. Skip the extravagant emotional band-aids and bare your hearts to each other instead.

Many of us struggle to communicate effectively. We desperately want our partners to hear and understand us, but we fail to truly listen and make space for their perspective too. We're so focused on making our point and being right that communication breaks down entirely.

The truth is, we can't force people to see things our way, no matter how 'correct' we may be. What the other person actually hears often differs from what we try to convey. Misunderstandings happen, good intentions get tangled.

Even the most enlightened among us mess up and thoughtlessly hurt those we love. It's inevitable – a question of 'when', not 'if'. When repeated, these moments of frustration can snowball into toxic patterns.

The key lies in changing our own responses. While we can't control our partner's behaviour, we can break free of any harmful loops we perpetuate. By shifting our responses, the dynamic itself transforms.

Below I'll describe some common destructive cycles and how to reroute them through conscious communication. The goal is self-awareness – to notice when we slip into toxic roles so we can catch ourselves. The only way forward is by owning our part.

Passive-aggressive behaviour

You feel angry with your partner but you show it in a hidden way instead of addressing it head on. You might make jokes about something you don't like, give them the silent treatment, or deliver sly, sarcastic digs.

Although your partner can tell you are annoyed, they don't know exactly why. Your behaviour definitely isn't doing anything to fix the problem.

Instead, be honest with yourself about how you feel. When you express it to your partner, you can use tact and restraint, without laying blame, and offering suggestions instead of making demands.

Ignoring the issues

When you brush something under the carpet, it will only get bigger over time. Avoidance can seem like an easier option, rather than potential conflict, but those issues will be back tomorrow.

Many couples never get to the bottom of their issues, because one or both are avoiding facing the problem. We have a range of coping strategies – learned over the course of a lifetime – to avoid having to deal with problems, for example: going quiet, working too much or using alcohol to numb the pain. Or we rush into major commitments, falsely hoping more bonding will rescue the relationship. For instance, having a child to rekindle fading closeness.

Although these escapes can seem like the easy way out at the time, they won't improve your relationship. Instead of running away from your fears, be bold and face the issues head on to help uncover root problems without blame – even if that means seeking counsel.

Seeking attention

When the lines of communication within a couple are down, people try to get the attention of their partners in different ways.

Your partner might openly flirt with others in front of you, or demand that you go everywhere together. Here, they are trying to tell you that they feel insecure and even worried about being abandoned. It can also be an emotional cue that they don't feel desired by you or that the relationship lacks quality time.

Explain to them that you will be there for them, and show that in your actions, giving them the reassurance that will allow them to change the way they act. If it's you who's seeking attention, try to find out where that insecurity is coming from.

Manipulating

Manipulative behaviour includes using guilt, avoidance or playing the victim to control outcomes.

All of us are capable of acting in manipulative ways, whether consciously or not.

Have you ever given your partner the silent treatment, shutting them out for days rather than simply explaining why you're hurt? Perhaps it's your partner who goes quiet on you, and when you ask them what's wrong, they say things like 'You must not care about this relationship if you can't even figure out why I'm mad.' Or, 'Forget it, you wouldn't understand.'

This type of response can make the other person feel guilty and anxious that they did something terribly wrong.

It's also manipulative to use vague statements, guilt trips and evasiveness to put the responsibility of your feelings solely on your partner, rather than owning your part.

You've probably heard of gaslighting before. It's where someone is led to question their perception of reality by another person, who purposefully manipulates the victim to make them believe that their judgement is wrong. This is a common tactic used by manipulators to make themselves look innocent.

When either or both people in the relationship are manipulative, it's going to be a game of cat and mouse, with each one trying to get the other to bend to their will. You have to nip it in the bud before it goes too far. Open up the discussion with your partner and explain how they are making you feel. Talk about why you are acting this way, even if you aren't sure where it's coming from.

Create a new dance

Instead of the terrible tango, create a caring waltz.

When you learn new steps together, the result will be more graceful. It will take time, but you can begin by saying things like, 'I feel upset with you, even though it might not be because of anything you've done. Can I just share it with you anyway?'

You can also offer a safety net for your partner by saying, 'You seem annoyed with me and I'd like to talk it through. Can we do that when you feel able to?' Then give them the respect to choose the time and place to talk.

As long as you're establishing room for dialogue, issues that were once deeply buried can beautifully come out into the sunlight. It can be the beginning of a deep connection as you help each other to find harmony together.

Knowing that every one of us makes mistakes means we can stop berating ourselves when they happen. Instead, focus on how you can take accountability and make amends.

As you go through the process of talking and listening, you might discover that it's just a case of you or your partner wanting to have feelings acknowledged. It doesn't mean that the other person will have all the answers, or has to come up with solutions. The answers will come in time, just as you will perfect your dance steps together, building a stronger bond as each day goes by.

A sign of maturity is when you review your actions after every single disagreement that you have, so you can grow as a person.

You will disagree, but do it fairly

Every relationship consists of two individuals at different stages of consciousness. To evolve together, you must be willing to resolve together – that includes anything that is unhealed within. This is how a relationship matures.

Sometimes, we treat intimate relationships as if they are the place to showcase our worst characteristics. We might behave one way with friends, or at work, or even among strangers – but all our etiquette goes out the window when we get into that cosy couple situation.

If you wouldn't snap at your colleague, sulk in a corner when out with friends, or speak harshly to someone you hardly know – why would you act like that with (or put up with it from) your partner?

In intimate relationships more vulnerability exists. There is no need to hide true feelings and tensions when you feel a sense of comfort and security. This closeness can lead you to express frustrations more openly than in other social situations. You may also believe that your partner will love and accept you despite displaying less favourable traits.

Things that we repress inside us in our professional life suddenly come out in the relative safety of the home environment. The deep tension in the body that goes along with ego identity finds a place to release, and if your partner challenges you, the ego can roar like a fierce creature because it feels threatened. To protect itself and to remain in control during these confrontations, it might attack them. It might happen suddenly and unexpectedly. If you're on autopilot mode, or if your inner awareness is dim, this is more likely.

When you're mindful of your own demons and those of your partner, it's possible to form a deeper connection. If you can act from the heart instead of from the ego, you stop caring about being right all the time, or 'winning' the next argument.

Resolving disagreements fair and square

When some couples come to a disagreement, they may feel the need to resolve issues right away to save the relationship. After all, communication is key to sustaining a healthy connection.

But if either of you is highly triggered and in fight-or-flight mode, you'll be unable to approach the conversation from a place of genuine curiosity, understanding, non-judgement, patience and empathy. And when that happens, the issue escalates, new problems are created and you both come off feeling even worse.

Bad communication styles can cause relationships to break down. So, although it's important to talk to each other, bad communication essentially puts your relationship on the ropes (see page 205, the Four Horsemen).

Emotional regulation must take place first so you can create a safe space to talk to one another, communicate respectfully, and work through your differences to come to a solution. Chaos doesn't create harmony – calmness does. It is the feeling of inner tension that makes us use defence mechanisms. The way to get past them, essentially, is to relax deeply, and be our authentic, caring and inquisitive selves.

As someone wise once said, when our hearts are distantly apart, we shout louder to cover the distance and be heard. But when our hearts are closer together, there is no need to angrily raise our voices to be heard.

So next time you find yourself in conflict with your partner, try a different approach. Agree to a break, practise self-soothing (perhaps through breathing techniques or going on a mindful walk), then set yourselves half an hour, or a reasonable assigned timeframe, to discuss the disagreement. This will hopefully set you up to approach the talk with calmness, which will close the distance between your hearts.

Make it clear from the outset that this time will be a chance for both of you to express your opinion and to hear each other out without interrupting one another.

When the allotted time is up, end the discussion and agree to reflect on what the other person has said. Then come back to it together later – again, set aside time for this – to see what you have both learned and if there are any insights you have both gained.

Navigating disagreements face to face

Not seeing eye to eye on everything is a sign of two unique individuals who are challenging each other's perspective. This can be a healthy dynamic that helps you to learn and grow; not everything has to be a battle of wills about who's right and who's wrong.

If you begin from a place of genuine care and respect for your partner, you have to accept that there will be differences of opinion. Rather than becoming either overbearing or passive, there are ways to de-escalate conflict and solve the problem. Here are some tools that can help you:

Start listening instead of talking

But listen with your heart, not only your ears. There's no need to negate their opinions or belittle what they believe, even if you don't agree with it. Instead of thinking about what you're going to say in reply, stop thinking and listen. That opens the ears of the heart.

Show that you're listening – and check you've heard it properly – by reflecting back what you've heard or mirroring the complaint: 'So, what you're saying is . . .'

Keep an open mind

You aren't judge and jury in your relationship and you don't need to reach a verdict. Maybe you are both right, or both wrong – and who cares? What's more important is that you make room for dialogue as you move towards a place of mutual respect and understanding. As you're talking, both of your worlds are expanding – so why contract the heart?

Take responsibility and stay on topic

Acknowledge and take responsibility for what you did or said that is upsetting your partner. Focus on the present point and resist the urge to bring up past events.

Be mindful of your body language

Avoid dismissive body language that will only escalate the situation. Rolling your eyes is disrespectful and hurtful – it says, 'What you're feeling doesn't matter to me.' Crossing your arms closes you off emotionally. And looking around the room or at distractions signals that you're not really present or listening.

Be your own referee

Stop the game when you see a foul. Or agree to disagree before it even gets there. No one likes dirty players, and even if you score a goal, at what price does that come? Follow the rules of fair play – whether you think you are right or not. Take an extra time-out to calm things down and regroup – that's better than letting things get out of control.

The rules you create around arguing and communications are only powerful when you uphold those rules. Even when things get heated, self-awareness has to call the shots so the fight doesn't derail and become unproductive.

It's not always easy to find your way back to each other after an argument. And even if you do, the cause of the triggers often goes unresolved. You might bury the hurt but stop seeing your partner in the same positive light. Subtle shifts in the relationship can go unnoticed until the next flare-up, with no one fully aware of the harm they are doing to themselves, or to each other.

The more attuned you are to your emotions, the more you'll be able to understand your reactions and why a conversation triggers an outburst. Calm, accepting presence and self-awareness is a great asset here. It's always within your power to be compassionate – the surest route to defusing a heated situation.

Relationship goals:

Two people who love each other unconditionally and not only share a vision for the future, but also support one another's dreams in the hope that they both shine.

PART FOUR

The Realities of Relationships

Love is only present when you are

Unconditional love means giving love now,
in this moment, of our own free will,
and expecting nothing in return.

When you move past the initial excitement of the honeymoon stage in a relationship, and settle into something steadier and more routine, you might start to notice questions arising. Have I made the right choice? Do I really love them? How do I know if this is love?

Rather than asking *what* love is, we might ask *when* it is.

The experience of love becomes more obvious when we do that.

Love lives in the now. Not in memories or dreams, and never in tomorrow.

Deliberate, conscious presence brings a special quality into life and relationships. There's certainly no shortage of distractions, so in the special moments where we can sit in silent observation, we can feel that quality, bone deep, zinging through our nervous system. Nothing in our outward circumstances needs to change, but inwardly, intentional presence opens us up to new depth, and that changes our whole experience of the moment, including the experience of our relationship.

Presence moves our focus from what's missing in life to all that we have right now, and all that someone is. When the focus is on what and who we have, it cannot simultaneously be on what's wrong and what's missing. It moves from the fiction of what we imagine into the reality of what is here. We know we are not present in love when we're demanding something imaginary from the other person.

Too often we don't love the person in front of us, we love the thought of them based on the image in our head. True presence means meeting them where they are, not where we fantasize they could be.

Love in the present moment doesn't concern itself with what was or what might be. It is accepting of all that is – including the real human being in front of us, just as they are. This is why love is often defined as a profound acceptance of who someone is. It has no hidden agenda.

You might think infidelity or poor communication are the main reasons people break up. But more often than not, it's distractions that cause relationships to fizzle out. Like death by a thousand paper cuts, these tiny, seemingly insignificant moments of presence missing from our day-to-day lead to a lifetime of separation and distance. Even when the other person is right in front of you.

Distractions lead to destruction

We can't fix others with thoughts and words. What we can 'fix' is our connection to presence. Mostly, a partner just needs us to show up with compassionate acceptance, rather than judgement or expectations. Real transformation happens by meeting each other as we are.

To fully experience the present and the people in it, we need to be able to focus on the moment.

In our digital world, focusing is harder than ever because we are masters of distraction. That's all we seem to practise these days, and the more we repeat something, the better we become at it. Distraction has become a habit.

How many times have you watched a movie while you're also on your phone? Even if you're not on your phone, you could be preoccupied with your thoughts. You could be reviewing and analyzing previous scenes in your mind, reflecting on what is now the past. Or you could be thinking about what might happen next, in the future.

Are you even watching and enjoying the movie, or are you just letting it play in the background? Now replace movies with life and people. Are you even experiencing your life and the people in it, or are you letting them play out in the background?

We can be physically situated somewhere, such as a social gathering, and our attention may still be on what's happening tomorrow. We're somewhere else. Our attention is absent from the present, the only real moment that exists. We are absent from reality. After all, yesterday and tomorrow are simply fragments of our imagination. You will only ever experience now.

So put your phone down more often. Make eye contact. Have long-form conversations. Practise deep contemplation and other focus exercises. Give gratitude for how things are without the need to compare them to the past or look forward to the future. Love others as they are. Love you as you are. And return to the flowing reality of the present moment over and over again as often as possible.

How to practise presence

Just as we train a muscle, we can train ourselves to develop focus, without making our lives harder. You are already present – so just remind yourself to step back into what you are, when you are, and where you are. Step out of your mind, back into reality.

Use moments that are already happening in your life as opportunities to give your undivided attention. It doesn't matter if those moments are painful or happy. Both kinds of moments work well.

So, when Debbie from HR launches into a detailed update of her keto diet, instead of allowing our minds to wander faster than a puppy with the zoomies, challenge yourself to focus on being fully engaged for at least a minute. Actively listen for at least 60 seconds. Really focus on her enthusiasm, the office sounds behind her, the funny way she gestures.

Then continue to repeat this from time to time during the day. When having dinner, focus on the cutlery and food in front of you – use all five senses to enhance the experience. Simply observe, without feeding into the mind's tendencies to judge or draw conclusions. Wherever you are – be there fully.

Remember, the key is to observe the moment for as long as possible. Experience what is right here with you without naming or labelling anything, without putting feelings or sensations into any kind of box – and here you are.

Doing this only a few times a day, for a few minutes, will help you develop your ability to focus and be present. Just as distraction is effortless, we can make focus effortless. Eventually, after cultivating this new habit, returning to the present moment comes with ease. The beauty of it is that you don't have to change a single thing, apart from placing your awareness more intentionally on what is happening in each moment.

A long-term relationship will die and be reborn a thousand times. It doesn't matter how long you are with someone, rather how willing you are to stay open to the new versions of them (and yourself) that are certain to arise.

You plus me actually equals three

There are three parts to a successful relationship:

You

Your partner

Both of you as a couple

If you want a solid relationship, you've got to realize there are three of you in the mix: you, your partner and the magical 'us' that you create together.

In Part One, I used the image of your relationship as a garden – one that both you and your partner have to tend to if the bond between you is going to continue to grow.

When the garden doesn't receive care, when there is no sunshine, or too much of it, when there are too many bugs, or not enough water, it can cut off the energy that nurtures the love we've cultivated. This could be the stress of our everyday lives – like weeds in our garden. The actions we take can nurture love again.

Yet caring for the garden falls short if the gardeners neglect caring for themselves and each other. When the tender gets tired, the tomato plants won't get watered. Our capacity to give depends on nurturing our own soil first.

The garden will struggle if only one partner consistently gives while the other withdraws.

The magic of growth, flowering and fruiting happens spontaneously, naturally and all by itself, but the conditions need to be right. We can't force the plants to grow. We can't plant stones and expect roses to come up. We can only tend the garden with care.

What does a balanced partnership look like?

While both you and your partner are responsible for feeding your relationship, it's not always realistic to expect a perfectly balanced, 50–50 distribution of effort and support.

There are times when one partner may face mental or physical health challenges or experience moments of discomfort or difficulty. During these periods, it's normal and healthy for partners to take turns stepping up and compensating for each other's needs.

I prefer to think of 50–50 as a reflection of the equal *commitment* both of you have towards sustaining and nurturing your connection.

Now the emphasis is on your mutual dedication to working together and supporting each other through various ups and downs, rather than strictly dividing tasks or responsibilities equally at all times.

This understanding acknowledges that relationships require flexibility and adaptability, with each partner giving their best when the other needs additional support, creating a sense of reciprocity and balance in the long run.

Some might suggest that aiming for a 100–100 commitment would be more fitting. But let's step away from the confines of numbers altogether.

Values like '100' have a way of tricking our minds into believing in the myth of perfection, completeness, flawlessness. But relationships are inherently human, and they ebb and flow. To disregard our humanity for the sake of giving our all will only invite guilt, anger and poor mental health.

Rather than focusing on percentages, it's healthier to simply commit to showing up the best you can each day, depending on your needs in that moment. But communicate openly so your partner understands where you stand and how they can provide support.

Avoid scorekeeping or tallying up what you've each contributed. This can breed resentment and competition rather than genuine care. Focus on supporting each other with authentic love.

Teamwork is key here, with both players looking out for each other. The couple complement each other while recognizing the other's strengths and accepting their weaknesses. Both are heavily invested in helping the other to fulfil their goals and dreams and will come together to solve problems. They are aware of failings in their relationship and will work to revitalize it in a caring, compassionate way.

Love needs actions that replenish the essence of your relationship. It requires you to check in more often, be present and create a shared story. It's about doing things that cultivate togetherness, not separateness. And it requires a committed practice of being curious about what it means to love and be loved.

Connection is work, not just a feeling

Healthy relationships are a privilege.
It's an honour to have someone to love and a
blessing to find someone who enjoys your goofy
impressions, corny dad jokes and eclectic clothing style.

I started this book by telling you that love is being, and relationships are doing.

The feelings of love you experience need to make way for actions that help you sustain a relationship. If we don't put the effort into nurturing a strong, committed bond through our actions, the relationship can't sustain itself.

The sad reality is that many couples who live together drift into a state where they're no longer feeling the richness of love – especially if they've been together for a long time. Although they might not argue much, there's little by way of connection, and indifference dominates. Rather than sharing their lives, they simply share a house. Any chemistry they had has long gone and differences once ignored are now creating distance. Conversations are kept to a minimum as each player withdraws and expects the relationship to run on autopilot.

Every day you wake up is an opportunity to choose your partner. Everything you do is either adding or taking away from the quality of your relationship. This isn't pressure; this is a privilege.

How to cultivate togetherness

Here are some practical choices you can make to nurture your relationship.

Be your partner's cheerleader

Let them know you are there to support them when they strive to achieve their dreams. Participate in their dream-chasing and show them they can spread their wings without fear of losing you. Find ways to be flexible in your plans and agree on mutual compromises so that you don't run the risk of sacrificing your own dreams in order to fulfil theirs.

Share meaningful rituals

Make plans to do things you both enjoy and generate excitement about them as they approach. Share time where you are focused on each other, like a weekly date night to cook a fun recipe together, or visiting a new coffee shop on Sundays.

Shake up the routine before you both get bored with predictability

Instead of telling your partner you love them just before you go to sleep, tell them when they are brushing their teeth or having a shave. There doesn't have to be a set time to express love, so keep it coming any time of day and not just at bedtime. That's just one example – think of other daily habits or patterns you've fallen into and how you might change them up to inject some energy into your relationship.

Be physically close to your partner

Sit next to them at home, hold their hand in the street, offer to give them a massage . . . and be clear that not all touch is about initiating sex. Human touch cultivates a great sense of belonging and bonding, as well as having a soothing effect and reducing stress.

Keep your story alive

Talk through the changes it has undergone, including all of the ups and downs. Keep the conversation going about what attracted you to your partner initially, why you love them and how you see your relationship growing in the future. Let them know how important they are and show that through your actions.

Be ready to make compromises

In any partnership, you've got to find that sweet spot of give and take, or else you'll find yourselves arguing about the most mundane things.

Compromises can go a bit like this:

> Them: 'Hey, let's take a selfie together.'

> You: 'Really? Do we have to?'

(And yet, you find yourself posing anyway.)

> Them: 'Can you come to this event with me?'

> You: 'Any other dudes gonna be there?'

> Them: 'Um, maybe.'

(Fast forward, and guess who's the lone guy in the room?)

> Them: 'Could you snap a pic for me?'

[A hundred photos later]

> Them: 'Why didn't you notice that one hair sticking out? You'll have to redo them!'

(With a sigh, you reluctantly keep snapping away.)

Approaching these moments with gratitude and love can turn seemingly insignificant requests and favours into opportunities to show up for your partner and make them feel acknowledged.

What a blessing it is that someone trusts and enjoys us enough that they choose us. That they seek our attention, and affection, and offer enough vulnerability to share their needs with us. Instead of being resentful, we can recognize that we also have someone ready to do our bidding too.

You will find that tiny compromises and gestures do far more for your relationship than grand, romantic displays of love. They are simple, but they are impactful, and they set the tone for when dealing with conflict. Because you've learned the dance of give and take, balance shows up in all areas of the union.

This is how you harmonize the boundless love at the centre of our being with all those details on the surface of reality. The details show up as a reflection of that silent, radiant presence. Life feels real again, your relationship reflects that centre point, and you feel real too, right in the middle of it all.

Suddenly, compromise seems like the wrong word for the things we do for the ones we love.

Anyone can treat you right for a short period of time, but it takes a special person to continue to give to the relationship for the rest of your life. That takes a lot of love and commitment.

You won't have perfection every day

Healthy relationships aren't always glamorous.
No matter how much you're in love, you are bound
to experience conflict, resistance, hurt and
destabilizing moments. Precious relationships
allow you to see the worst side of yourself
and your partner but still choose love.

Even with the person you love by your side, you or they might experience doubt, indifference, boredom and irritation. And you'll have a need for space, no matter how much you want to be together.

It's possible to feel more attracted to your partner on some days than on others, just as you will feel more or less attractive depending on your mood. This doesn't mean you love each other any less.

These are the daily ins and outs of being human that often lead to disagreements, tensions and conflict, which are important to work through.

Marital expert and researcher Dr John Gottman identifies four kinds of relationship conflicts that predict break-ups within couples – he calls them the Four Horsemen. They are: criticism, stone-walling, defensiveness and contempt.

Through observational research, Gottman also discovered a 5:1 'magic ratio' in healthy relationships. This suggests that for every negative interaction during conflict, a healthy marriage has five or more positive interactions. So if there have been five negative interactions, you'd need at least twenty-five positive ones to balance it out. The higher the ratio, the better the relationship.

Let's explore the Four Horsemen and see how these conflicts can be turned into more positive interactions, using examples based on conversations I've had with some of my followers and friends.

Converting criticism into compassion

Jaz: I really love Kiera, but it upsets me when she criticizes me all the time. If I forget to take out the rubbish, she calls me lazy. Even when I buy her gifts, she complains that I've bought the wrong colour. To be honest, it seems like I can't do anything right.

When your partner attacks you for who you are, it's hurtful. They're supposed to support you, but instead they are pulling you down.

For a relationship to work, you have to start from compassion and work through your differences together. There will be things going on with Kiera that are making her behave this way, and Jaz also needs to think about which triggers her behaviour is setting off in him.

When you find yourself in a situation where your partner is complaining, it can touch a nerve, but if someone is just plain mean, that's a different story. Abuse in a relationship can be both emotional and physical and you should never have to put up with either. Being triggered and being abused are completely different. Abuse is intentional and intolerable.

However, if the critical behaviour seems out of character, meet it with curiosity about the fear or hurt beneath it.

You can set the intention to listen while still maintaining boundaries. Make clear that you want to understand their viewpoint but you won't accept abuse. Through openness, judgements can unwind to reveal hidden wounds wanting care on both sides.

Compassion has a unique way of disarming someone who is temporarily unable to navigate their thoughts and feelings while projecting criticism. But loving, patient energy can turn the entire scenario around. Even though their attitude spoiled the moment, love helps you transform it into a learning opportunity. Loving compassion may switch a hostile exchange into a safe place where you better understand each other's frustrations.

If you feel your self-worth is being attacked or that you are being criticized for who you are, you might be tempted to hope things will change. But ignoring your emotional well-being is never a good idea. It comes at a high price. Nothing is going to change within your relationship if only one of you is trying.

Sidestepping stonewalling with vulnerability

Kelly: Jasmin keeps stonewalling me every time we have a disagreement. She'll storm out of the room, refuse to talk to me for days and give me the cold shoulder. When things have calmed down, she acts as if it was all my fault and expects me to apologize. I've had enough.

Jasmin may never have learned how to communicate her emotions, or she may be dealing with something that she can't even understand herself. Her behaviour is hurtful to Kelly, who truly loves her and wants to stay, but she's feeling locked out and rejected. Stonewalling is one of the main reasons that couples break up, and this is understandable.

When the walls go up, how can you even begin to communicate?

If your partner shuts you out and isn't prepared to do the work to open up, how long should you wait?

Sometimes this kind of behaviour is manipulative, coercing you into apologizing or making you feel guilty for something you haven't done in order to get back to normal. If, after offering your support, you feel that your integrity is being compromised, you need to think about what the future will look like.

Fortunately, much of the time stonewalling is a learned behaviour pattern that can stem from someone who never felt like their voice mattered. At an early age, the ones who were meant to love them would deny their reality or shut them up. They rarely had strong examples of healthy communication and conflict resolution.

Remember, you aren't meant to fix a partner's pain-patterns, but with love, together you can re-learn what it means to talk after a disagreement.

If you can extend vulnerability and be patient enough to honour their fear of communicating, your response to your partner's stonewalling can be a chance for an important emotional breakthrough. Assure them their opinion matters, even if it challenges your own. Help them feel safe enough to open up. Remind them that you're here to listen. Empathy, understanding and boundaries will take down a stonewaller, brick by brick.

Diverting defensiveness with trust

Sharmi: Did you make the reservation for tomorrow at the restaurant like I asked?

Izaac: Jeez! Do you know how busy I've been at work today? Why didn't you just do it yourself!

Attack is the best form of defence, right? After being caught out by your partner, it's natural to want to strike back and defend yourself. Then you can declare all-out war!

When couples engage in this kind of tit-for-tat exchange, things can get out of control. If your partner acts defensively even though they haven't been attacked, it may be the sign that they don't have the emotional tools to be accountable for their actions.

It might appear they aren't invested in the relationship, making out that everything is your fault. If you take on that blame, it's like admitting that you did something wrong. As the conflict escalates, you'll find it increasingly difficult to nurture a caring partnership.

Defensive behaviour can occur when your partner has a victim mentality or is unable to assume accountability. These behaviours often stem from a deeper issue – identifying too much with their thoughts and ego. The defensiveness comes from the ego, not the person's true Self. Deep down, there is never anything to defend. What is defending itself is really a condition of mind – like a scary, uncomfortable tension in the body and the nerves, conditioned through repetition and habit. It's not the real person at all.

When you see your partner become defensive, take a step back. Their nervous system is activated and their inner child feels challenged – even when you are not there to compete or spar with your lover. As soon as you see that guard come up, it's your signal to use love to disarm them and diffuse the situation – but only if you have the patience to in the moment; if not, try later.

Defensive statements can be the projection of a stressful day, or they can reflect years of resentment. Either way, it's going to take inner work to explore why your partner feels attacked. Remind each other that it is you two versus the problem, not versus each other. Never engage in defensive banter. It is best to walk away if you're not ready to lead them back to a calm state of mind.

Defusing contempt with communication

Jayden: I used to be a strong, independent person, and now Max is making me feel worthless. He laughed when I told him I was thinking of going for a promotion and said, 'What makes you think they'll give you the job? You don't even know how to turn on a computer.' I don't know how much longer I can go on like this.

When your partner is sarcastic, puts you down or mocks you, their comments will eventually eat away at your self-worth. I'm not talking about harmless banter here, which has its boundaries and isn't usually meant to offend. When someone adopts a morally superior position, it stems from a desire to cover up their own inadequacies or to have control. Someone who feels the need to belittle you is someone who secretly feels small and powerless inside.

This kind of behaviour doesn't appear overnight – it's a long build-up of negativity over time and can become a common pattern in a relationship.

Contempt between couples is one of the main reasons for break-ups. It expresses condescension, hostility and the 'I'm better than you' model.

If you want a relationship in which you both support each other on the journey to self-love, healing and happiness, there is no room for contempt. The more self-awareness you gain, the less this kind of behaviour will interest you, or even make sense to you.

Overcoming contempt can be challenging. This is usually because it has years' worth of dry wood to fuel the raging fire. It's kept notes of wrongdoings and the scoreboard is never in your favour. So be cautious when attempting to smother the flames.

Invite your partner to open up about how you've hurt them. Don't retaliate with a list of wrongdoings they've done. If you've invited them to speak and offered to listen, it's critical that's what you do.

Take accountability for how you've made them feel. Share how important it is to you to get this right. Forgive them for fault-finding, and forgive yourself in the process, without carrying guilt or shame as baggage. The unconditional love at the centre of our being is a solvent, like water, washing away the past and nurturing new growth at the same time.

Finally, agree to talk to each other when something's gone wrong. Don't bury hurt inside and let it fester. Addressing unhealthy patterns in the relationship should be a top priority.

Happy couples aren't just the ones posting kissing selfies. They're the ones having uncomfortable conversations, helping each other overcome trauma and ugly-crying to save their relationship. Happy couples prioritize growth and are a source of inspiration for each other.

You will have to forgive often

Forgive them, not because their actions were okay, but because you deserve peace of mind. Let go of the hurt so you can heal and move forward with your life, even if it's without them.

We've all been hurt by loved ones. Whether it was a thoughtless comment, broken promise or act of betrayal, these wounds cut deep. When someone wrongs us, we naturally tend to personalize the experience, as if their behaviour was somehow a reflection of us.

Our natural reaction might be to retaliate, hold resentment or abruptly end the relationship. However, the healthiest relationships practise genuine forgiveness regularly. Making mistakes is a part of being human, and sometimes we can hurt people unintentionally.

What is forgiveness? It's not excusing, denying or even forgetting the offence or action. True forgiveness means freeing yourself from the negative emotional experience and the egoic desire to punish the one who wronged you.

In a relationship, it's understanding that our partner cannot always love from the centre of their being, even if they are committed to cultivating love, because the ego-mind gets in the way. Perspective offers power here. Instead of viewing yourself as the person knocked to the ground, you see it as being bumped by someone who tripped. Staring at your scraped knee gives you limited perspective on what's happened.

Forgiveness is also valuing the relationship over the specific action that hurt us. Forgiveness is as much for you as the other person – it allows you to move on from the pain and give relationships a chance to heal and reconnect.

Accept first, then let go

Forgiveness doesn't happen instantly. The ego identifies strongly with being right and righteous. Admitting wrongdoing or letting go of anger threatens the ego's need to see itself as superior and morally correct. Paradoxically, being a victim also keeps the ego feeling like it's on top.

Navigating forgiveness becomes especially challenging when faced with individuals who refuse to acknowledge their role in causing hurt and offer no apologies for their behaviour. For serious transgressions, the road is long and difficult, especially if we heavily identify with the pain.

The first milestone on the step to forgiveness is acceptance – acknowledging the reality of the situation before you can process the emotional hurt. As clinical psychologist Harriet Lerner states, 'We do not have to like it or approve of it, but accepting reality is the first step in improving it or changing how we respond.'

True forgiveness requires releasing anger and the desire for retaliation. Consider the context and factors that may have influenced the other person's actions. Recognize that we all make mistakes. The question becomes – is the relationship more valuable than this singular offence? Can you live with the apology that was or wasn't offered?

Forgiveness also means letting go of holding the wrong against them. You cannot use guilt as a weapon down the road or use your partner's past faults to excuse your own behaviour. It requires starting from scratch with a clean slate.

Where to draw the line?

Forgiveness doesn't mean you have to stay in unhealthy relationships. Sometimes, the wisest thing you can do is forgive someone, but know that they don't need to play an active role in your life.

One topic that comes up often when considering forgiveness is infidelity. Do you forgive them for cheating?

For some people, cheating warrants an automatic end to the romantic relationship. For others, it may be something they can overcome, if the cheater expresses genuine remorse and commits to rebuilding broken trust. There are no universal rules here – it depends entirely on your personal beliefs around monogamy and your read of the situation.

Some couples come back stronger when a spouse has had an affair, while others just can't weather that storm. It really depends on how you personally feel about it and whether you can put infidelity to one side.

What I would like to say, though, is that trust is a two-way street. If your partner has been unfaithful, can you trust yourself not to keep bringing it up for the next ten years, every time you have an argument? From the moment you accept what happened and decide to move on together, you both have to create a fair playing field where there are no fouls or dirty tactics. Are you prepared to do that?

Loving someone can mean accepting their errors and failures, in the same way that they accept yours. There doesn't always have to be an either/or ultimatum, and we can exercise compassion after the event. You can build something new, with the transgression actually revealing what was missing in your relationship and allowing you to fix it.

I'm not trying to condone or condemn infidelity here. What I want to focus on is how to re-establish trust, if that's what you want. You might need to move boundaries, alter habits and rearrange the furniture as you work to rebuild from the beginning. But before embarking on any of that, you must trust yourself.

- Can you come to terms with your feelings and move forward?

- Can you talk things through with your partner without spitting out accusations, criticism and judgement?

- Can you listen without prejudice?

- Can you take responsibility, if it was you who cheated?

- Can you understand what was behind your actions?

- Can you express your needs and hear the needs of your partner?

- Can those needs be met?

- Can you keep the promises that you make to each other from now on?

Forgiveness is a personal choice. It can be an incredibly healing gift we give to ourselves and others. However, you must weigh up each situation and know when enough is enough.

Consider if this was an isolated event or part of a destructive pattern. Our memories can bias recent harms over years of shared joy. If this seems like an aberration from normal behaviour, it may be easier to exercise forgiveness and keep investing in the relationship.

When someone does something that hurts us, we can reflect on whether or not they have been committed to loving us from the centre of their being. Upon reflection, a recent hurtful action might create a deeper revelation – consistent ways your partner has been coming from a place of non-love. When our actions have been coming from a place of love, it's easy to notice where love is lacking. After all, radiant love can expose where love is obstructed and reveals imbalances. Here, you might see that the relationship is not reciprocal.

Trust actions over words. If this relationship diminishes your light, makes you feel unsafe or no longer serves your growth, forgiveness will not change that. You owe it to yourself to walk away. More on this later.

Emotional maturity looks like having a disagreement without shaming, blaming, name-calling or projecting your trauma onto someone else.

Boredom isn't bad

*We often perceive good people and steady
relationships as 'boring' when we've grown
accustomed to turmoil. After constant ups and
downs, stability feels unfamiliar – our minds equate
drama with passion. But peace and balance
are signs of a thriving relationship.*

Relationships aren't an Instagram highlight reel, as much as we try to pretend. There's usually no music swelling when you go in for a kiss, just the weird slurping sound your lips make. No beautiful sunset backlighting your tender embrace, only the flickering fridge light as you battle over the last yogurt. You won't capture soulful gazes while playing with an adorable puppy, just your partner's death stare when you forget to buy dog food again.

Sure, there are healthy doses of romance and intimacy, but for the most part, a healthy relationship is resilient, enduring, balanced, consistent, stable and sometimes boring.

A little bit of boredom doesn't have to ring alarm bells – but it is an invitation to get curious.

If you're accustomed to dramatic relationships, peace feels odd at first. Your body links love to the intense highs and lows. So stability might feel flat, even boring, apparently void of passion and excitement.

This happens because chaotic relationships keep your nervous system fired up with constant uncertainty and crises. You get addicted to the rush, for better or worse.

When a healthy connection lacks this drama, you don't get the same chemical reaction – and withdrawal sets in. Your body misses the emotional rollercoaster, even though your spirit yearns for calm.

Until that conditioning changes, the brain overrides the heart's true longing. What you're used to trumps what's good for you. Healing means retraining your system to associate love with steadiness rather than just drama.

Of course, in some cases, boredom can be a sign of stagnation. The difference will be that boredom isn't the only dynamic shift you're experiencing. If the connection is fading, then other energetic changes will occur too, like a lack of attention, apathy and emotional distance.

Boredom alone isn't something to worry about – and could be a sign of health and maturity between you.

Building stability

Many relationship professionals can predict the longevity and quality of a connection based on a single factor: how the couples respond to each other's bids for connection.

A bid for connection is any action that invites the other person to participate in a shared moment. When your partner sends you a funny video, or suggests you cook together that evening, or reaches out to hold your hand when you're walking down the street, these are all bids for connection.

In each scenario you have a choice about how to respond: do you watch and acknowledge the video – or leave them on read? Do you say yes to cooking together and seek out a new recipe to try – or roll your eyes at them for suggesting it? Do you take their hand and give it a squeeze – or pretend you didn't see it?

How about your partner – do they turn towards or away from you when you seek attention, confirmation and affirmation through positive and polite means?

Responding to these small bids is a way of acknowledging the other and investing in the relationship. While not thrilling or glamorous, presence and participation in one another's life is an indication that you're in a stable, secure and loving relationship.

Inner recalibration

Your nervous system might be attracted to a push-pull dynamic, where you are regularly invited for closeness and then dismissed. Your body might recognize love by the intense range of emotions someone makes you feel. Here are some ways to remedy these chemical misfires, find safety in boredom and let your partner in on your experience.

- Without placing blame or responsibility, open up to your partner about how a lack of drama is unfamiliar. Together you can find healthy ways to spark excitement or invite them to support your healing journey by allowing them to show you new, stable ways to feel love, closeness and intimacy.

- Create more awareness with self-inquiry. When you begin questioning the relationship because it's less 'thrilling' than others you have been in, get to the root of it by creating a Good vs. Bad list. Evaluate the long-term relationship attributes you value most (for example, commitment, honesty, growth, shared values) and compare them to what would result from cheap thrills (drama, uncertainty, disloyalty).

- Accept that unhealed parts of your heart and biochemistry crave the intensity of relationship drama. Then call it for what it really is – abuse, neglect, breadcrumbing, instability, unreliability, dishonesty and immaturity. Whether it was a caretaker or a previous relationship, someone may have loved you wrong, and it's time to retrain your heart, mind and body.

Finally, remember that there is tremendous joy in peacefully, wholeheartedly and intentionally doing nothing at all. We think joy only comes from outings, from activities, from making new friends and going to new places – and so to sit and do nothing seems utterly boring. In fact, it is a way to find a tremendously rewarding dimension of being human. It can help reconnect us to depths of ourselves we've completely forgotten and ignored. It can help bring a calm and meditative balance back into the hectic, stressful life that threatens our relationship. We can learn to make friends with our silent, open and expansive heart, and in doing that, bring a balm of healing and peace into the relationship too.

You're a partner,
not a babysitter or parent

You are not your partner's saviour. Supporting their growth is vital, yet you cannot walk their path for them. True care involves stepping back, allowing them to be their own person, and gently nurturing their growth from a place of compassion, understanding and trust.

There's a difference between, on the one hand, *caring* for someone, and on the other, *guarding* their emotions and well-being.

Caring for someone is healthy. Hopefully, it's a mutual kind of care – you and the other person value one another's health and happiness, and you're there for each other.

But sometimes, care can drift off-course and turn into a form of guarding. You withhold your own emotions and needs from that person because you feel they're not equipped to deal with your truth. You take care of certain aspects of their life (for example, you might look after all the finances or household admin on your partner's behalf) because you feel like they can't handle doing it themselves. You avoid telling them bad news because you think the stress will be too much for them.

And of course, there are times where it's necessary to withhold sharing terrible news. For example, after a major loss or trauma, in times of serious physical illness or injury, in cases of depression and anxiety, or for neurodiverse conditions like ADHD or autism.

The key is meeting the person where they're at. Additional caregiving is meant to nurture growth and eventual autonomy when ready. Too much guarding and caretaking isn't good for either of you. It sets up a dynamic where you've become the babysitter or parent and they've become the child.

But even the most vigilant parents must eventually let go as their toddler learns to walk. The child must test those wobbly legs. Occasional stumbles on the carpet strengthen still-developing muscles that will one day stride confidently.

We too must gracefully allow our partners to stumble and rise. Guide, but don't control. Advise, but don't command. Support, but don't disable their journey.

Guarding restricts their freedom to be independent and stand on their own two feet, and it restricts your right to an equal and mutually fulfilling relationship.

Stepping back from old roles

If, as you read this, you see that you've begun to take on the role of guarding your partner in a relationship, then I encourage you to take a step back. You need to reclaim your status as capable, emotionally valued human beings who both have needs and strength.

Ask yourself these questions:

- Does this feel like a relationship (whether that be a romantic partnership, friendship or family relationship) between two adults who are responsible for their own realities, their own mindsets, their own bodies?

- By trying to guard or protect the other person, are you limiting their ability to grow?

- What are you getting out of caretaking in this way? What deep need does it fulfil for you?

- If you were in an equal relationship with this person (or with someone else), would that push you to grow and confront your own limitations in ways that make you feel uncomfortable?

And stepping into new ones

If you've become a guard or caretaker, then you've taken your focus off yourself. Whether only in this relationship, or more generally, you're putting your energy into helping and caring for someone you perceive to be less capable than you.

In doing so, you're giving yourself an excuse not to work on your own growth. Not to acknowledge your own limitations. And not to consider what you might need to change in order to become the person you wish you could be.

So, shift the focus back to yourself. Instead of assuming your partner isn't up to hearing your truth or handling their own challenges, start to open up.

Allow them to see you; allow yourself to become vulnerable; and allow them to be in charge of their own emotions and reactions.

The paradox of the inner journey in life is that as we realize and value the oneness of all things, we also see the value of the individual. Part of our journey involves the painful separation from the family and tribe to become complete, whole and unique beings, able to take care of ourselves. When we mature as unique beings, bringing our own gifts to the collective, the whole Universe celebrates our contribution with us.

Acknowledge their pain,
don't try to fix it

*Deep listening is more valuable than
giving advice.*

In a world where so many speak their mind and share their opinions, the act of saying nothing and just listening has become an art form.

When we speak, it's all about us. How intelligent, spiritual, eloquent, witty, informed and authoritative or inspiring we are. Our words represent our thoughts, beliefs, persona, perspectives and so many other facets of our being.

But listening? Listening has everything to do with others. It's an offering of time, space and other emotional resources that we extend to others. It's an invitation to be seen, felt, heard and understood. It's a pause from our own point of awareness to take a peek into someone else's.

To listen is to lean into empathy, offering undivided attention, asking questions and probing the other person to continue sharing, being supportive, being non-judgemental and sending welcoming nonverbal messages through expressions and body language.

Your whole being is saying, 'I'm here, listening carefully to every word you say.'

Funnily enough, when people come to you with their problems, they usually don't come to you for the wise words and advice you offer, but for the safe space you've made for them to pour out their heart and bare their soul.

Begin by asking them if they're looking for guidance or just a supportive ear to vent their feelings. If it's the latter, unpin your life coach badge and make yourself comfy.

How to hold space

When you hold space for your partner, you can be fully present without feeling the need to impose your will. Some of the ways in which you can practise holding space include:

Listening deeply

This is not just about hearing what someone says, but listening to understand. Listen with your heart. There's no need to agree or disagree – although validating their feelings with simple nods can be helpful. It's all about allowing them to express themselves without fear of criticism or judgement. Everyone's experience is valid, and by acknowledging their feelings without judgement, you create an atmosphere of acceptance.

Making room for your partner

Most people feel like they have nowhere to go when they want to cry. You can be that place and allow your partner to unload anything they feel: sorrows, worries, doubts, fears, pain. Sometimes, all it takes is for you to listen and acknowledge what they are experiencing.

Cultivating empathy

Step into your partner's shoes and view the world through their eyes. Cultivate empathy by understanding their experiences, fears and joys. When you can genuinely grasp their perspective, your responses become more compassionate and considerate. Empathy is the bridge that connects hearts, fostering a deeper connection.

Freeing yourself from the urge to fix the situation

As mentioned above, giving advice or making helpful suggestions might come naturally, but not everyone wants that. They might just need a safe space to unload how they feel without feedback. Often, we need to work things out for ourselves. Being told, 'You should do this or that,' can make us feel like our problems are being swept under the carpet or that we aren't being heard.

Establishing boundaries

While holding space involves openness, it's crucial to establish healthy boundaries. Clearly communicate your own limits and respect those of your partner. Boundaries create a secure framework within which both individuals can express themselves freely without fear of overstepping each other's emotional or physical comfort zones.

The quiet, nurturing energy that is the source of our being supports us in this way. It allows us to have all our experiences, whether uplifting or gruelling, without judging us as successes or as failures. Practising steady compassion in our romantic relationship helps us remain close to the source of love in our hearts.

Real relationship goals can't be found on social media

Remember, your grass will never get greener by focusing on someone else's lawn. And sometimes you might compare your lawn to someone else's without realizing that their grass isn't even real.

I once attended an event where a couple were locked in a verbal cage match, hurling insults and threats like pro wrestlers. At one point, they charged towards one another full of rage, ready to let their arms swing wild. Only the swift intervention of the security guards stopped them. I had never witnessed anything quite like it, especially between a couple.

Days later, while scrolling through Instagram, a suggested post caught my eye – it had evidently gone viral. The image showed a beautiful couple, gazing dreamily at each other. 'They look so in love,' I thought. Delving into the comments, it became clear that everyone was in agreement:

‘OMG, you guys are goals.’
‘I want a love like this.’
‘You two are made for each other.’

Something about the picture struck me as familiar. Perhaps it was the setting: I was certain I had been to the location where they captured that moment. Zooming in, while trying my absolute best not to accidentally 'like' the image by double-tapping, it hit me: this was the same couple who I'd seen engaged in the bitter confrontation at the event – the picture was taken on that very day and posted afterwards.

It struck me how people were forming 'relationship goals' based solely on a picture, completely oblivious to the actual dynamics of the relationship. No one would ever guess this duo had been escorted out by security just moments after this picture was taken. Had they witnessed it, I'm not so sure they would be aspiring to such a relationship.

We associate 'relationship goals' with a snapshot of a happy couple. But forming a goal out of a glimpse can encourage misleading expectations.

What do real relationship goals look like?

Well, let's scrap the social media images first.

Let's take looks out of the equation, too. External beauty is subjective, and looks fade. What's more, looks can quickly lose their charm when someone is muttering abuse or displaying acts of cruelty. Some would describe this as a turn-off.

Every relationship is different, and there's no external model you should be following, even if society can make us feel that way. It's more important to pay attention to how you feel in the relationship, and how it honours your needs and allows you space to grow than it is to use external benchmarks.

What you will find is that a meaningful and mindful relationship is one that is RICH – an acronym for the four pillars of Respect, Intimacy, Communication and Honesty. By implementing these, you have a great chance at sustaining a precious bond.

Respect

Maintain respect in every action towards and conversation with each other and yourself. This is especially important when you're at odds or emotionally charged. Basically, at times when it's most challenging to uphold.

Intimacy

Intimacy isn't just a by-product of a relationship – it's something you have to invest in if you're going to keep it alive. Honour intimacy to establish emotional and physical closeness. Don't let long talks and deep conversations fade simply because you think you know each other well. There is always more to discover about yourselves and one another. And if sex is important to you, keep that fire alive, even if you have to try out different things to reignite passion.

Communication

Speak often about what's working, what isn't, and how you feel. Don't assume or try to make your partner guess. Keep respect in mind, too, as you communicate. Allow both of you to be seen, heard and understood.

Honesty

Be honest in the process, even if it means having difficult conversations. Honesty ensures we are making the right decisions for ourselves and the needs of the relationship.

Marriage as a goal

Society often assumes that marriage is an end goal for everyone – and in some cultures, this is strongly embedded in the blueprint for a happy and successful life. Nevertheless, marriage is right for some people, but not for everyone.

Relationships and marriages require work, patience and understanding. Sometimes we pick a partner and rush marriage for the wrong reasons – only to find ourselves stuck, confused and even dreading our lives. And this burden can feel even heavier when you have kids.

None of these are strong enough reasons to get married:

- All your friends are getting married.
- You want kids or already have a child.
- Family members keep telling you that you're getting old.
- You feel like you need someone to be by your side to live your best life.
- You feel like something is wrong with you because you're still single.
- You want to feel complete and heal through someone else.
- You are afraid of being alone forever.
- You feel like a failure for not being married.
- Everyone on social media is getting engaged – and they look happy.

Of course, you don't need to be fully healed (or perfect in any sense) to enter a relationship or a marriage. While it's OK to desire a healthy connection, don't expect someone else to be the answer to all the challenges in your life.

Don't expect someone else to be your source of happiness.

Don't expect to live a fairy tale once you find someone to journey with.

Don't expect people will celebrate you, leave you alone or stop judging you because you're now married. The truth is, if there are unresolved conflicts within, a partner will probably bring them to the surface (often unintentionally). And it's here that you'll realize the power of a healthy, devoted partner who wants to work with you rather than against you.

And remember, marriage or kids might not be your end goal, and that's OK. Love is a human instinct and spiritual endeavour and is not confined to certificates.

Your truest, deepest joy, fulfilment and contentment is already home, in the centre of your heart. Your relationship will be an extension and a continuation of whatever you carry inside. Use the relationship to clear that space and reveal joy.

If you are considering the idea of marriage, do it because you see a future with someone, not because you're alone, unhappy, feeling left out or pressured by parents. A marriage doesn't take all of your troubles away; it often amplifies internal conflicts. So pick your life partner carefully.

PART FIVE

Letting Go With Grace

Relationships need freedom to blossom

Like air, love can't be held. You can't bottle it,
claim it, hide it or own it. You can't demand it,
buy it, manufacture it or think it into existence.
All you can do is be it.

In Part One, I introduced the idea of practising non-attachment as a way of freeing ourselves from suffering.

The risk of a happy, healthy, fully invested relationship is losing it. This fear keeps many of us from realizing our potential and capacity for connection. But that's the nature of life. The risk of presence is absence. Even light has no meaning without darkness with which to compare it.

Instead of embracing the totality of an experience, we tarnish the best parts of it by worrying about its impermanent nature.

Instead of relishing our relationships, we can obsess over the idea of losing them.

This shows up in relationships when we cling to someone. Instead of offering a loving non-attachment that creates space for two individuals to choose each other over and over again, we clutch them in our grip with the false idea that the tighter we hold on to them, the longer they'll stay – and the longer our happiness will stay.

Non-attachment in a committed relationship is a liberating experience. It is the full expression of shared love. Structured by boundaries and compassionate communication, it exists under a premise that I will never need you, but I will always love you. And may you never need me, but always love me.

Attachment says: 'I need you' and 'I want you'.

Love says: 'I am me, you are you, and I enjoy sharing this space, where love lives, with you. I will not make my emotions your responsibility. I will support your expansion as I do my own. And I remain curious about you and the development of our connection.'

We can appreciate the beautiful colour and fragrance of a flower. It can inspire a feeling of love and joy within us, but if we hold that flower in the wrong way, squeezing it tightly and clenching our fist around it, the flower loses all its charm. Whereas if we gently cupped it in open hands, we would let it share its beauty freely. We can never possess the beauty of that flower; we can only admire it.

Releasing fearful holding on makes space for growth. Loosening your grip brings the flower and your hand relief.

Healthy bonds, like flowers, blossom beautifully when given freedom. Open hands allow mutual flourishing.

Attachment maintains an iron grip. When attached, it's easy to project love onto a partner and assume you wouldn't feel love without them there. This isn't love, it is based in fear. Fear drives attachment and blocks authentic love from showing up.

It's normal to fear losing someone who contributes to your happiness. Even as children, we get upset when someone takes away our toys that we love so much. A maturing of love allows us to become wise and to appreciate the moments of joy in our lives, without demanding ownership.

What does non-attachment mean in a loving, committed relationship?

Non-attachment isn't indifference, apathy or a lack of love. Nor does it diminish desire, interest or intensity of emotions. Some people believe non-attachment means to be 'emotionally numb'. Some people even become obsessed with the idea of non-attachment, and, ironically, create an attachment to the concept without noticing.

Where there is non-attachment in relationships, there is the freedom to be yourselves and to fully enjoy each other for who you are, not what the other wants you to be. No more having to perform or please to feel loved. There is only authentic love that nurtures growth and joy.

The real root of non-attachment is being secure in yourself. There's a profound sense of security in knowing that there's an innate core, or Self, deep within you, which is unaffected by change, even if everything else in our life is fleeting.

Not even our bodies are ours; we're simply the drivers behind the body, like we are of our cars. We must care for our cars so they can continue to function in a healthy way, but they don't define who we are. This understanding is essential to practising non-attachment.

When your relationship is based on non-attachment:

- Your focus is on giving love, rather than getting validation.
- Your motivation for being in the relationship is compassion and joy, rather than fear or insecurity.
- Your attitude towards your partner is accepting and allowing, rather than controlling or possessing.

- The communication between you is honest and understanding, rather than blaming or manipulating.

- Your boundaries are healthy and independent, rather than weak and enmeshed.

- Your happiness and self-worth come from within, and don't depend on the other person.

- Problems become opportunities to grow, rather than destabilizing forces.

- You see your partner as an independent subject, not an object to claim ownership of.

- And your connection is freeing and reciprocal, rather than suffocating or sacrificing.

Your needs are your own

We can share our needs with a partner, and motivated by love they might attempt to meet them. But *nobody* else is responsible for your needs. If you're expecting someone else to fill a void in you, you are likely to be disappointed.

Your partner can give you emotional satisfaction and make you feel contented, excited and blissful. But what happens when they don't? Do you feel frustrated, hurt, confused, unloved?

We all have different emotional needs and also show our emotions in a multitude of ways. Your partner might give you the companionship, communication, trust, affection and sex you want, but they may not be capable of more. What if you crave mental stimulation, financial security, tenderness, respect, a confidant?

Nowadays, we expect one person to give us everything we need. It's impossible for anyone to meet all of our needs, and we can't load them onto one individual.

It's a lot healthier to have outlets with other people who can give you what you want, be that friends, family or colleagues. That doesn't make your relationship with your partner any less meaningful. The opposite is the case – it makes it more durable and rewarding.

You can't be everything for your partner. Nor should you make them your absolute everything.

How to love without attaching

Attachment doesn't only restrict the space for love to blossom in relationships, it hinders all chances of you experiencing love from others, yourself and the Universe. Love is meant to flow freely like a river, but attachment adds stones and blockades that keep it from pouring into and out of your heart. Riddled with expectation, fear and lack, love's current slows or becomes chaotic and unpredictable.

Here are some pointers for loving without attachment:

- Don't project a role or storyline onto your partner. For example, don't expect them to be your 'rescuer' who will finally heal your childhood wounds and meet needs that no one else could.

- Stay present, stay curious. Keep interest alive by embracing who your partner is now versus who they were when you first met.

- Reject co-dependence and maintain a strong sense of self. Keep nurturing individual friendships, hobbies and dreams outside the relationship.

- Maintain healthy standards, not unhealthy expectations. Communicate needs without demanding that your partner meets every romantic fantasy.

- Address which needs to meet and which to share. For example, you may handle finances solo but meet intimacy needs together.

- Remain vulnerable, open and honest. Reveal emerging struggles early before resentment builds.

- Remove guilt and shame from the connection. If you stumble, apologize then move on, rather than punish yourself.

- Ask but don't expect. Request support without requiring partners to always deliver solutions.

- Love them, not what they do. Value who they are beneath their roles, behaviours and actions.

- Love yourself and not what you offer. Feel worthy beyond what gifts and resources you provide.

- Accept impermanence and release fear. Embrace natural changes in personality and priorities over time.

Loving without attaching only feels foreign because we're often so fear-driven in our connection. A sense of happiness carries with it the dread of when we might become sad, angry or discouraged again. Yet with enough surrender, trust and practice, love will help you transcend the ego stories and conditioning that we have learned about in previous chapters.

Commit to the process. This is one of the most profound ways to unblock your heart and welcome love into your life.

Let go.

Love rushes in when you allow it.

Being with the wrong person makes you feel less like yourself

Love is a source of growth, not constant sacrifice.
If a relationship isn't inspiring more wins, it's a loss.
Life is far too short to betray your needs for the sake
of making it last or to avoid the embarrassment
of walking away. You tried – and that's enough.

Relationships are in a constant state of flux, morphing from one day to the next. Events come along and challenge the dynamic – for example, having children, prolonged illness, a move, the loss of a family member, financial shifts, an affair. And, as individuals, we also change as we go through life.

Love can fluctuate in its intensity. When it starts to wane, that doesn't mean it never existed. It has simply faded for this particular person or circumstance.

Your heart, body and mind are exceptionally intuitive. They know when a relationship is no longer working.

The question is, how long will you stay when you see that it's not?

Consider how often you make excuses for your partner. Maybe you've always wanted children, but three years into the marriage they tell you parenthood isn't for them. Do you sacrifice this lifelong desire for the sake of love? This is simply sacrificing yourself.

Authentic love would say, 'We don't want the same things anymore and, because I honour you and I honour myself, this is goodbye.'

Knowing when to move on

When they're no longer right for you, it'll feel wrong most of the time. Your heart will constantly feel heavy, and you'll notice yourself change just to uphold the relationship.

Before you make any decisions, tune into your inner needs and see if they are being satisfied. I'm not talking about how much your partner pampers you, or how often they take you out. I'm referring to those deep emotional needs where you feel respected, honoured and loved for who you are.

You can be so in love with the past, their promises and their potential that you forget about what's happening in the present.

But the closer you are to yourself, the harder it will be to betray your needs and go against your desire for a stable, healthy, happy relationship.

It's not your job to change your partner, nor for them to change you, although you may have spent some time doing just that. You might have more emotional maturity or be more connected to your spirituality while your partner is in a different place. If you really feel that the differences are making you suffer, you must accept the reality and go from there.

I wish I could tell you that every problem can be resolved. Unfortunately, that's another myth. The reality is that we won't necessarily be with our current partner in five, ten or twenty years, no matter how committed you are.

Remember: you still have the capacity to love greatly, even after a relationship has run its course, because love never leaves you.

Stop accepting breadcrumbs when you deserve a whole cake

A single question can help you realize if a relationship is right for you. Ask yourself: 'If I wanted my child to experience the fullness of love, would I want them to be in this type of relationship?' This works whether you have children or not.

When you've invested your time and energy in a long-term relationship, the thought of losing that can be scary. You might tell yourself that it's better to stay than to be alone, that you have built a life together and can't face the alternative. You could even say that you love your partner and can't imagine life without them.

It can be easier to go on, following the daily routine you've both become accustomed to, enjoying an intimate moment here or there. You might even make a great team, both working together to raise a family. It's possible that you are best friends, helping and supporting each other when needed. And if you have children, splitting up may never be an option as you feel the cost would be too much on their stability. You could stay with your partner because you are financially dependent on them, or because they are the only love you've ever known. You might also stay because you have nowhere else to go or the alternatives just aren't feasible.

When you aren't aware and accepting of the love you deserve, and don't maintain spiritual and emotional independence, a self-serving partner can prey on these insecurities.

By offering you breadcrumbs – just enough to get by – you find yourself staying longer, waiting, wishing and hoping that someday soon they'll offer more. You become a prisoner to the promise of 'maybe one day'.

It may take some time, but eventually you must realize that there is no more that they can offer. And in that moment, my hope is that you will choose yourself and walk away.

If you're weighing up whether to stay or go, here are some questions you can ask yourself to make more informed choices:

- Are you able to stay true to your deepest values within the relationship?

- Does your partner honour your principles, even if they don't agree with them?

- Are you able to maintain your independence and autonomy?

- Are you able to work through and resolve conflicts together?

- Does your intuition tell you that you're on the right track?

- Do you feel your emotional needs and desires are adequately prioritized?

- Do they make you feel as seen, heard and desired as you make them?

- Is there mutual effort to connect and foster romance and intimacy?

- Is there a steady commitment to growth, both as individuals and within the relationship?

It's also wise to consider how your relationship choices would differ if . . .

- You had never been hurt in the past?

- Your self-esteem was higher?

- You felt more comfortable and content being alone?

- You felt like you didn't think there was anything inherently wrong with you? (Not to be confused with unhealthy patterns of behaviour.)

- You had faith in the future?

- You were independent?

Consider a lifetime perspective too. One day, we'll each have to let go of this physical life, including everyone we love. We practise non-attachment by letting go of the unchangeable past and unpredictable future.

This may sound bleak, but it releases us to fully receive the gift of now. Each moment, though fleeting, offers beauty if we are fully present.

Don't relinquish life cheaply, losing precious hours or energy to fantasy, resentment or fear. Instead, channel love and awareness into the current riches before you.

What will you do with this moment that will never come again? Will you waste it, or will you awaken to it?

Not every relationship will last. But at one point, every relationship made you laugh, smile and love in ways you hadn't before. It's not about lasting forever. It's about savouring every moment before you say any potential goodbyes.

Sometimes we have to leave the ones we love

A sign that you need to move on from someone is that you no longer feel safe around them.

Imagine you share a home with your partner. One way you express love is by cooking dinner to nourish them. But instead of accepting the food, every day your partner takes the plate you offer them and throws it to the floor, trashing the kitchen in the process.

In that extreme example, it's clear that your expression of love is not being reciprocated. Worse still, it's potentially putting your safety at risk.

But there are lots of ways – not all of them so obvious – in which your offer of love might be rejected or used against you.

When another person's actions do not nurture your own connection to the source of love at the centre of your being, it makes it harder to love them unconditionally. As your inner light becomes dim, all you can think about is your safety and survival – protecting yourself.

Moving out, or otherwise putting some distance between you, might allow you to continue loving them unconditionally – albeit from afar. For as long as you remain connected to the centre of your being, the distance between you won't hinder your capacity to reach for unconditional love in the present moment.

By staying and enabling abuse, you can't guarantee they will love you from the same centre. Just as a nurturing home has basic standards of mutual care and respect, so must a relationship. Unconditional love persists, but its healthiest expressions involve reciprocal nourishment rather than one-sided damage.

Unconditional love is boundless, but it isn't binding. You aren't forced to continue to offer love in a relationship when your basic needs aren't being met.

If you feel harmed by someone and they aren't willing to repair that damage, you need to draw a line.

When harm masquerades as love

Unfortunately, we can end up in relationships with people whose priorities are self-serving and who don't have our best interests at heart. You've probably heard the term 'narcissism', which refers to a personality disorder that gives people an extremely high sense of self-importance, making them ignore the needs of those around them.

Yet nowadays, people often use the term narcissism loosely to describe narcissistic tendencies, rather than clinically diagnosed Narcissistic Personality Disorder.

Whether they are a narcissist or have tendencies, abusers can have you questioning your self-worth and leave you feeling unsure of who or what to believe.

If you recognize several of the characteristics below in someone, it might signal you are connecting with a manipulator, and potentially a narcissist, creating a toxic environment for you and the relationship.

It's worth reiterating that while abusers exhibit many of these behaviours regularly, most people will display a few of these from time to time as an unaware ego-defence, yet not be a persistent abuser. Pay attention to the frequency, intensity and combination of these behaviours, as well as their impact on your well-being.

Excessive self-centredness

- They prioritize their own needs, desires and feelings above all else, leaving little room for your needs or feelings.

- They demand excessive praise and validation from others to maintain their self-esteem. They employ all sorts of cunning tactics to have their emotional needs met. They constantly need to boost their ego.

- They often exaggerate their achievements and talents, sometimes to an unrealistic degree, to appear superior.

- Conversations with them often revolve around them, and they may show little interest in your life or thoughts.

Lacking in empathy

- They struggle to genuinely understand or care about your emotions and may dismiss your concerns or feelings as unimportant.

- They use your emotions and vulnerabilities against you, exploiting your weaknesses to their advantage.

- They use affection and validation to control or punish your behaviour.

Entitled and demanding

- They act entitled to special treatment and become angry or resentful when they don't get what they believe they deserve.

- They have unrealistic expectations of you and your relationship, setting you up for failure.

Manipulative and controlling

- Known as love-bombing, they shower you with excessive affection, attention, gifts and compliments to gain control and establish emotional dependence, only to later withdraw those behaviours, leaving you confused and insecure.

- They use manipulation tactics such as gaslighting, guilt-tripping or playing the victim to control you and make you doubt your own perceptions.

- They disrespect your personal boundaries, both emotional and physical, and expect you to do the same.

- They isolate you from friends and family to gain more control over you and limit external influences.

- They often deflect blame onto others, which makes holding them accountable for their actions challenging.

- They switch between affection and cruelty, making you uncertain about their true intentions and keeping you emotionally invested.

- They create drama and jealousy by involving a third party, causing confusion and insecurity in the relationship.

- They use passive-aggressive language, sarcasm or double meanings to confuse or control you.

Insecure and defensive

- They can't handle criticism or feedback, often reacting defensively, becoming angry, or giving the silent treatment.

- They project their flaws and insecurities onto others, accusing you of what they are guilty of.

- You feel afraid to express your true feelings or thoughts due to the fear of anger or retaliation from them.

Escaping from abuse

If you feel you are being abused, you need to get out, as the situation could seriously harm your well-being. You should never stay in a relationship that is stripping away your self-esteem. At the end of the day, only you know what you are prepared to put up with and if it is in alignment with your self-worth.

When you commit to a person who isn't committed to themselves, you run the risk of compromising yourself. The first steps are acknowledging you deserve better treatment, believing in your ability to break free, and educating yourself on these key tools for safely identifying and releasing yourself from an abusive partner.

For more help and information, please talk to a doctor, health visitor or midwife. Alternatively, in the UK, women can call the freephone National Domestic Abuse Helpline, run by Refuge, on 0808 2000 247, or email helpline@womensaid.org.uk. Men can call Men's Advice Line on 0808 8010 327, visit the webchat at Men's Advice Line or call ManKind on 0182 3334 244.

If you identify as LGBT+ you can call Galop on 0800 999 5428 for emotional and practical support. Additionally, anyone can call

Karma Nirvana on 0800 5999 247 for advice on forced marriage and honour crimes.

If it is an emergency, you should always call 999.

If you live outside of the UK, you can usually seek the advice of a healthcare professional or contact a local charity specializing in domestic abuse.

When they're no longer right for you, it'll feel wrong most of the time. Like an incessant ache in your heart, you'll notice yourself change. Your spirit shrinks, your sparkle dulls and you find yourself faking a smile. Being with the wrong person makes you feel less like yourself, and may lead you to seek validation from them that you are enough.

Letting go won't hurt as much as holding on to an illusion

When we realize that the person we love isn't quite right for us, it's not the truth that hurts; it's having our illusion destroyed.

Falling for someone's representative best self is like having a crush on Iron Man but then dating regular ol' Robert Downey Jr. Sure, he's still a great guy and looks slick in a suit, but he's probably not going to fly you around in a hi-tech rocket or save the world before dinner.

It's easy to hold on to the idea of someone, but that's just a temporary, moving picture.

Idealization is the act of holding on to a fantasy image of someone based solely on their potential and on your personal expectations – and it's a common phenomenon in relationships. Idealization might involve overlooking or downplaying the partner's flaws or negative qualities, creating a version that doesn't match up with who they truly are. When the rose-tinted glasses come off, and the partner fails to meet these idealized expectations, it can lead to heart-shattering disappointment.

The idea can be appealing – to focus on someone's best bits, invest in their potential and root for their growth or transformation. But it can also mean we're not enjoying that person as they are, but rather as we wish them to be or in the moments of promise they display. Often, we want our partner to change so we don't have to – so we can avoid facing our traumas, wounds and insecurities. So that we can stay put and hope to feel secure in their presence. The changes we seek in others often reflect the neglected aspects of ourselves.

Here are some behaviours or beliefs that suggest you might be idealizing a partner or relationship:

- You minimize or justify their flaws, harmful behaviours, lies or inconsistencies.

- You fantasize about how 'perfect' things will be once they change or mature.

- You make excuses for their inappropriate actions.

- You feel responsible for 'saving' or 'fixing' them.

- You pressure them to improve or live up to their 'potential'.

- You cling to rare moments of dream-like connection as the norm.

- You nostalgically dwell on the exciting honeymoon period.

- You imagine how you'll feel once they finally commit in the way you want.

- You fault yourself when they mistreat you or let you down.

- You keep thinking you can't bear the grief if you leave them.

- Your self-worth comes from winning their love.

- You distrust reality checks from concerned friends or family about them.

- You avoid reflecting honestly on the relationship's repetitive pain.

The purest and deepest love is full of acceptance, not expectation.

Living consciously means embracing reality rather than fantasy. It's continually letting go of made-up assumptions to see the awe-inspiring truths in front of you. We're able to act with wisdom when unclouded by illusion, which also means we're able to walk away from unhealthy relationships.

Which pain hurts more?

Heartbreaks hurt not only because we lose the person, but also because we lose our routines, plans, dreams, sense of security, livelihood and the comfort of familiarity. There's a lot to grieve, so give yourself the time, patience, compassion and space you need.

Letting go is never easy.

Ultimately, we mourn the death of a future we had played out in our head. We not only grieve the person, but also who we were when we were with them and how our life looked, the priceless shared moments, along with the glamourised ideal future. The present becomes hard as the pain of loss, filled with grief, haunts us.

There is certainly a lot of pain that comes with letting go, but by holding on to the illusion, you experience spirit-shrinking pain for longer. Here are some of the ways you might experience that pain:

- You experience bitter disappointment when your partner fails to fulfil impossible standards that only exist in your imagination.

- You sacrifice more and more of your needs, boundaries, values and truth to try to force an unrealistic fantasy.

- You make excuses for unacceptable behaviours while suppressing, minimizing or denying real problems.

- You give everything to 'fix' them into an idealized image that can never materialize.

- You feel increasingly frustrated, resentful and powerless when they don't change into your perfect vision.

- Growth becomes stunted as you pour energy into maintaining delusions rather than facing reality.

- You miss out on opportunities for real, rooted connections by clinging to surface-level dreams.

- Confusion and instability increase the longer you base your life decisions on illusions.

When we finally let go of a relationship, the pain can feel insurmountable. Our mind will often play tricks on us, suggesting it might have worked if only we'd tried harder – or that perhaps we didn't give them enough time to change.

However, by clinging to an illusion that the relationship could transform into our perfect fantasy, we sign up for deeper, prolonged suffering. The bitterness stings sharper each time our unrealistic expectations are denied.

At some point, we must open our eyes. We have a choice: to continue chasing shadows, losing more of our spirit along the way, or to take the brave step into the light of truth. The path of authenticity and self-love inspires us to let go, grieve the illusion and reconnect with reality.

Only by releasing fantasy can we build connections rooted in understanding, empathy and seeing ourselves and others clearly.

Once you make the step back into authentic heart connection, you won't believe how much time you wasted chasing an empty illusion.

The reality of love might not always look like it does in the movies, but it sure feels better when it's real.

Accept rejection.

Don't beg.

Never chase.

Know your worth.

Choose yourself.

Growth comes with goodbyes

Some things no longer belong in your life.
Let them go and trust that what comes next
will be better than what's just left.

As you evolve and expand, you will bid au revoir to many people, places and parts of yourself that no longer resonate with your new level of awareness. For the ego, this is the hardest part of life. It desperately wants to hold on to the familiar, even if it's a source of pain. Stepping into the unknown is a dangerous quest – big changes riddled with unpredictability scare the ego.

But non-attachment suggests you can love someone without needing to keep them. It doesn't create a sense of inner conflict when saying goodbye. Non-attachment accepts that everything is temporary, and things naturally come and go.

If you can release the urge to cling to what isn't working, you'll lessen the resistance and discomfort that occurs when things shift to what they're meant to be.

Goodbyes are inevitable, not to be feared and necessary for your growth. They become less uncomfortable with more non-attachment, but if you must hold tight to something, let it be your own heart.

Ground your energy so deeply within your heart space that you know saying goodbye to external things doesn't mean you lose anything. It can even symbolize that you are drawing closer to your true, authentic centre.

Continue to let go when your spirit urges you to. It simply means it's ready to make space for what comes next. Trust yourself. Release your grip. And ease into the ebb and flow of receiving and letting go.

Letting go of someone you love is no easy feat. If you have a deep attachment, it's even more challenging. But staying when you don't feel you belong means releasing something else: the chance for a healthier, happier relationship. It often includes denying some of your intrinsic needs. Staying can mean limiting the ways you could be experiencing true, unconditional love.

So, either way, a painful, unfulfilling relationship requires you to let go of something – them, or a part of yourself.

If you find yourself halfway out of the door, consider pondering these courage-generating questions:

- How will staying impact your self-esteem? Can you afford to lose any more of who you are for the sake of another?

- Will this relationship influence you to forsake your values? Are you really willing to abandon what you fundamentally believe in?

- Will this relationship strain other important relationships in your life? How can it not, if you are unhappy?

- Imagine someone you know who loves you unconditionally. What advice would they give you?

Healing your broken heart

Fully and authentically loving another is the most rewarding opportunity with the greatest risk. We expose the depths of our being in the hopes of being embraced – knowing that one day they may walk away and take a piece of us with them.

If you are suffering from heartbreak, you might be wondering what you did wrong, why your partner broke up with you, how they could be so cruel. I feel for you and know it can be a torturous experience.

People say it takes time to heal. That's only partly true. Just as often, the sands of time slowly sweep over our wounds, but the wounds themselves don't heal. This happens when we don't address what we have been through and instead allow all of that pain to sink into the deepest parts of our psyche without addressing it.

No one can heal without tending to their wounds with care and compassion. Rejections are invitations to love yourself more.

One of two things will occur after a heartbreak. We can close off and prevent further opportunities to be vulnerable, to love and be loved. In this case, our suffering never ends. Or we rip ourselves wide open, knowing that love may come and go. But because we choose to be an open vessel for love to fill, the risk remains worth it. The joy of connection outweighs the fear of loneliness, and the pleasure of presence surpasses the possibility of loss.

Healing isn't linear, but start by meeting your needs, from the basic necessities to the callings of your spirit. Heartbreak healing calls for tender treatment. Let the tears flow until the laughter comes. Let anger become understanding and sadness turn to acceptance until the attachment is released. Be patient with your heart, and surround yourself with love until you can embody it again wholeheartedly.

Heartbreak is a pivotal part of the human experience. We cannot control what comes and goes, but we can embrace and cherish what we have while we have it.

In my book *Healing Is the New High*, you'll find a step-by-step guide to approach your healing journey.

Never let boredom, loneliness or temporary suffering be the reason you go back to the people, places or circumstances that brought you down or drove you away.

Grieving makes space for renewal

You can decide to move on for the right reasons and still feel sad about it. It's not wrong to feel upset when you say goodbye to something that once held so much value in your life.

As we mentioned in a previous chapter, when we let go, we grieve. Grief is a normal human emotion that serves an evolutionary purpose. It is a feeling of loss: what we thought belonged to us is no more.

You might experience grief when you lose a person – or when you lose other things, such as a job, or plans that didn't come to fruition. When something treasured vanishes, we feel cut off and exposed. It's painful, but it can lead us to seek new connections, to heal and transform.

Accepting that we are no longer with our partner is heart-wrenching. It requires that we come to terms with reality. This means honouring our emotions without judgement and allowing them to manifest naturally. It's OK to say, 'I feel sad', and better to avoid thinking things like, 'I'm overreacting'. You deserve to go through this period of hurt and to take the time to look at why the relationship didn't work out.

Remember that an open wound won't heal if it is covered – it needs fresh air to help the cells regenerate, so don't deny yourself this. Be gentle and encourage a deeper understanding of yourself at this time; you need it.

Make space for your pain

When you are trying to get over a broken heart, allow space for your feelings. There's nothing wrong with recognizing you still feel hurt, but instead of letting those feelings of hurt put you into a state of paralysis, try to acknowledge them and bear witness to the fact.

As your tears flow, or your heart sinks, be mindful of the experience and feel the waves of emotion passing through you before letting them go. Try expressing how you feel out loud – you can do this on your own or in the presence of someone else. Maybe it will go something like this:

I feel so upset.
I never expected this relationship to end.
I still love them.

I can't bear being without them.

The pain is overwhelming
and I can't stop feeling miserable.
I feel so angry/disappointed/frustrated.

After you have acknowledged how you feel, allow yourself to reframe the narrative, if you can. If not, that's fine – these things aren't easy. But if you can, allow yourself space to observe your pain without harshness, something like:

It's natural to feel the way I do.

I still love them and I know that love is never wasted.
I will treasure the time we had together.

I know that the pain I'm experiencing now will be
replaced by happiness in time.

Self-love heals. Time helps, but it's facing those raw emotions that will make you more able to cope with any future relationship. You have every chance of coming through this with the clarity you need to enjoy a wonderful new relationship.

Don't rush the process

The grieving process can't be rushed. Taking time out can be really helpful. It will give you the chance to get things out of your system, like a detox, and you can focus solely on yourself. During this phase, you can try to figure out who you want to be in your next relationship and what you are prepared to bring to it.

Before you embark on a new relationship, figure out if you are ready.

Ask yourself:

- What's motivating me?
- What would be right for me?
- Can I bring my authentic self to this relationship?

These aren't easy questions to answer, but as long as you start the healing journey, you are on the right path.

The key is not moving on too fast. If you don't fully deal with the nuances of sadness that come from ending a relationship, it will become the emotional baggage that plagues all following connections.

Seek inner peace

Just as you need to have a regular intake of physical nutrients to keep your body healthy, you have to feed your emotional needs: anything from engaging in your favourite hobby to going out with friends. The best way to find inner peace is to discover it within you – in the silence behind your turbulent thoughts and emotions. Use the Hakalau meditation exercise on page 76 to do this. If you struggle to do that, it may help to try the following.

Instead of dwelling on what your ex may have told you in anger – or even on purpose – to hurt you, dwell on positive affirmations about yourself.

Write down your strengths and repeat them often, or note anything that shows you are a good person, such as simple acts of kindness you've demonstrated. These affirmations can be of help:

- I am full of love. I exude positivity and light. I am a source of goodness, which continues to come back to me in multiple ways.

- Letting go of what doesn't serve me becomes easier every day. I am constantly creating space for new and wonderful energy to enter my life.

- I am worthy of deep care, warm compassion and pure love. I acknowledge my wholeness and welcome beautiful souls into my life who match my level of awareness.

Not every relationship is destined to be permanent. While we crave companionship, warmth and compassion, which are all very human traits, we may not find them in every relationship.

But that shouldn't stop us from being willing to share and experience those emotions when they do come along.

We all have the gift of being able to love unconditionally and in abundance, although having a closed heart will hinder that immensely.

The pain we experience in relationships tells us something about ourselves – it tells us that we want, crave and need love. Hold on to that thought and let love be your guide. The centre of your heart is a dependable compass, because it is directly connected to the source of joy and peace – your pure, uncomplicated natural state of being.

The door to love is always open.

The Universe will replace
people who do not
reciprocate your love.

That is why love is never
lost, it is only found.

You can still look back with love

Even if you've grown apart or no longer speak, cherish those wonderful experiences and moments you had with them. At one point, they made you smile and laugh, and they supported your journey. You can always look back with gratitude in your heart.

If you've exhausted energy and time on someone who didn't appreciate you, you might find yourself looking back and thinking of yourself in all kinds of negative terms – naive, foolish, silly. You may have even asked yourself these questions:

How could I be so gullible that I fell for their games?
Why did I trust them and ignore the signs?

And if you find yourself missing someone who treated you disrespectfully, that might turn into something else you beat yourself up about. *What's wrong with me – why am I so stupid?*

You're not alone. We shouldn't feel bad or sorry for our acts of kindness and seeing the good in others. Yes, we can learn from these experiences and bolster self-love to create more harmonious relationships with less tolerance for harm in the future. Nevertheless, can we ever really be wrong for being good to others – even if they were 'wrong' for us at the time? After all, their actions are about them, and your actions represent you.

Don't regret being a good person with the wrong people. Your actions say everything about you, and their actions say everything about them.

Believing, trusting, appreciating, sharing and supporting are all traits of a compassionate being. Sure, you might have shown these qualities to someone dishonest and disrespectful. Still, their actions and incapacity to show gratitude for your energy does not take anything away from who you are. Can you imagine how much brighter and more tolerant the world would be if it was filled with your positivity, understanding and gentleness?

People are often doing the best they can with their conditioning, resources and belief systems. We don't need to turn cold to stay warm. We only need to remind ourselves that we have a lot of love to give – and one day, someone will treasure our energy and meet us with the same willingness to love wholeheartedly.

To see goodness in others is to possess goodness yourself. And once you recognize your inner light, the harder it becomes for someone to dim your spark by taking away your pride and dignity.

Never regret the love you shared

Relationships not only teach you how to love someone else, they also teach you how to love yourself. Every relationship can bring you closer to a deeper understanding of who you are, what you need, what you want and what you don't want from a partnership – and from life itself.

When connections break down, the ego goes into overdrive to cope. If your ego is defensive, it may repeat stories of how awful the other person was, how unsatisfied you were, how it was about time things ended. But villainizing isn't healing and can make it harder to move past pain. It can also create animosity, anger and regret – unhelpful emotions that may ripple into other areas of your life and keep you energetically tied to someone.

When anything ends in life, tuning in to your higher Self, love-consciousness, leads to gratitude. You'll recall why your energies merged in the first place, find appreciation for the experience, and, most importantly, integrate lessons from the relationship to move you closer to who you want to be as a person and where you want to go in life.

If you've walked away from an abusive situation, it might not feel like there is much to celebrate. It's hard to look at the emotional scars left behind and say, 'Wow, I'm grateful for these.' And that's valid. When appreciation for the situation feels fleeting, try to remind yourself there was growth. Because for a time you tolerated the incompatibility, then you chose self-love.

There is a place for anger and grief when we lose someone in this way. Hold space for it. And when you're ready, shift your focus towards appreciation, understanding and letting go to release suffering. Soon you will see that goodbyes serve a purpose in helping you grow, and invite authentic hellos.

The gift of self-forgiveness

At some point in healing your heartache, self-forgiveness is key.

Forgive yourself for staying so long, tolerating poor behaviour, wondering if you could've done more, not being able to 'save' them, lacking self-awareness – whatever it is you blame yourself for, release it, as many times as you need.

When you reflect on who you once were, how you once behaved and what you used to tolerate, don't allow shame to overcome you. Instead, give gratitude to your unconditional love for finally pulling you through.

If it was you who made a key mistake that led to the breakdown of your relationship, recognize how much you have grown since then. In that moment, you lacked the awareness or tools you have now. Your capacity to love has deepened. Honour the journey of your expansion and show yourself the same compassion you would a close friend. We all make mistakes on the winding path to conscious love.

One of the best gifts of undergoing your own transformation is understanding where others are in their journey – and having compassion for them.

It can be frustrating to watch people we care about, or even strangers, live in ways that don't serve their greatest good, just as you once did. Pity and judgement won't change a thing. But imagine what would have helped you when you were there, when you stayed too long in an unhealthy relationship, when you sold yourself short, when you settled for a life you dreaded because you feared the unknown. How would it have felt for someone to wrap their arms around you and tell you it would be OK?

Acceptance and appreciation are powerful ways to bring out the best in each other. No matter where others are in their healing, they deserve the space to be as they are. So be mindful when urging others to heal too. Demanding growth or forcing your path onto them only raises their defences. Their walls grow thicker as they retreat into old patterns.

But when you nurture the spirit of another, no matter their stage of healing, the walls soften, the eyes open, and they begin to notice in themselves all the parts of them that you've held space for – the same way you held space for your self-perceived broken parts until you loved them back together.

Heartbreak hurts. But it also shows you how to value yourself and be accountable for your own happiness.

Celebrating love on your own

Single doesn't always mean lonely. In the same way,
taken doesn't always mean loved.

You can live alone, without a partner, and still experience unconditional love. You might be giving a whole lot of love to others in
your life, be it friends, family, workmates, neighbours or the dogs
in the local shelter.

Our culture glorifies relationships and assumes something's wrong
with you if you're single. But if singlehood were understood as
what we first strive to succeed at, relationships would be healthier,
happier and more successful.

When we assume someone is lonely when they're single, or assume
they're loved and respected in a relationship, we see them from
our social conditioning – not from the reality of their story.

A person's relationship status won't reveal their well-being. People
can suffer silently in relationships that appear to be thriving. They
may also live out the life of their dreams all on their own. Similarly,

when people are single, they can celebrate the joy they cultivated together with an ex-partner, or healthily process longing for a new one.

What does this mean for you?

Whether you're coupled or feeling #foreveralone, know there is no right or wrong way you 'should' feel. 'I'm in a relationship, and I should be happy.' 'I'm single, and I should be dating.' No. The only thing worth recognizing and addressing is the authentic emotional experience that you're having.

Don't let social media tell you what your life must look like, based on your relationship status or otherwise.

Meet yourself where you're at. Your genuine emotions don't require a label. Don't judge them as good or bad. Just be a witness and stay curious about where they came from.

And, finally, know this: whether you are coupled or not, your well-being is always your most significant responsibility. Regular check-ins will help you prioritize your happiness and healing within and without a relationship.

Ways to cultivate love on your own

There are so many ways you can show yourself love and foster loving relationships with those around you.

Take yourself on dates or plan solo trips

Treat yourself to experiences you love, whether it's a movie night, a solo dinner at your favourite restaurant, or a weekend getaway to a dream destination. Enjoy your own company and create memories for yourself.

Leave yourself love notes

Write love notes to yourself, expressing gratitude for your strengths and affirming your worth. Place them in unexpected places, like your wallet or mirror, as delightful reminders of your self-love journey.

Extend love to your friends and family

Show appreciation to your loved ones by surprising them with thoughtful gestures or gifts. Share the positive energy that would typically go into a romantic partnership with those who matter to you, reinforcing the importance of meaningful connections.

Journal for self-reflection

Journal using prompts that expand your vulnerability and invite deeper self-compassion. Check out *The Greatest Self-Help Book (is the one written by you)*, a journal in which you'll find lots of prompts and exercises.

Commit to personal goals and objectives

Set and commit to personal goals that align with your passions and aspirations. Whether it's learning a new skill, starting a hobby or pursuing a long-held dream, dedicate time and effort to your personal growth.

Exercise creative expression

Explore your creative side through art, writing, music, dance, or any medium that resonates with you. Creative outlets provide a unique space for self-discovery and emotional release.

Connect with nature

Spend time outdoors, whether it's a leisurely walk in the park, a hike in the mountains or a day at the beach. Nature has a rejuvenating effect and offers a serene environment for self-reflection and relaxation.

Learn something new

Challenge yourself to acquire new knowledge or skills. Whether it's taking a course, learning a language or exploring a subject of interest, learning fosters personal development and a sense of accomplishment.

You're never single. You're always in a relationship with yourself – so stay committed to loving yourself and evolving.

Choose love

Love is unity and peace. Though we differ, it brings us closer. It creates space for compassion and understanding. Love dissolves fear and anger, clearing the way for solutions born of our shared hopes. Love is a force of healing. It energizes our spirits, nourishing our humanity. When so much divides, love reminds us of the truth that binds us. It is a light guiding us through the dark. It's one of the few things that we know we are doing right.

Choose love.

As our journey in this book comes to an end, the lifelong path of choosing love still lies ahead. The light of love lives within each one of us and is waiting to penetrate all aspects of life.

If you want a deeper appreciation of yourself, a more meaningful and authentic relationship, and to do your part in creating a more peaceful world, you'll have to make choosing love a habit. Here are practical ways you can integrate love into your day to day.

Validate others

Many people feel unseen, unheard and unwanted. But it takes so little to validate someone's experiences. Listening is a good start. Don't attempt to offer solutions, dismiss their feelings or share how the same thing has happened to you.

Be a mirror reflecting love and humanity. Confirm that how they feel is perfectly fine. See them, hear them and love them as they are.

Radical acceptance

When you stop seeing people for what they offer you and begin to seek who they really are, radical acceptance and genuine curiosity takes hold, creating an environment of pure love.

Find the best in others

Where your focus goes, attention grows. Imagine what a positive impact we'd have on each other if we hyper-fixated on the best in one another. When you actively look for and acknowledge people's talents, courage and acts of kindness, they will likely feel inspired to share even more of their light.

Practise genuine interest

There are many opportunities to help and support those around us. Embodying love doesn't mean you have to save the world, but getting outside of your own circumstances and taking interest in others will result in deeper connections and the expansion of universal, unconditional love.

Love gets the final word

Choosing love is like coming back home to a familiar, comforting place. Authentic love fits your soul like your favourite pair of jeans fits your body.

The love I have tried to describe in this book is not the idealized surface layer of appearances we see on social media memes, in movies and in romantic books. There are no roses raining down while orchestral music swells dramatically. It's not a popular drama or a cheesy sitcom.

It is quiet, and it is deep, and it is humble.

Like water, love takes on many graceful forms. It nurtures life. It dissolves and carries away harmful emotions and pain that may be lodged within us. It demands nothing, and clings to nothing. It claims no credit or fame. It teaches and heals all, without declaring to be anything special. We carry it with us as part of who we are.

This love is not a psychological theory, nor is it a complicated spiritual teaching – although it can seem so at times. It's not just a sentimental feeling, either. I don't believe anyone can fully put it into words. It cuts straight through all the myths we spin about relationships in such a simple, intuitive way. It is what it is, without excuses. It is the heart of us.

People don't always tell us what we need to know about love. But we can know love for ourselves when we consciously choose it – for us and for those we care for. We know it in the moment we deliberately share that feeling of 'I choose love', without hidden agendas, straight from the heart.

Choosing love means getting real and finding your way by tuning into your inner compass. It's trusting the magnetic pull you sense deep in your core without reservation or doubt. Choosing love means surrendering completely to where your heart points, letting it guide each step. You do this because you know love is truth, love is wise, and love is the only thing we can do right.

By making this choice, you come to embody love and move through the world with intention. You create ripples of understanding and care without a word.

The belonging and joy of a great relationship requires trust. A trust that the person opposite you will continue to express love from the centre in them that connects to the centre of you. It's trusting you share a bond on the soul level even when life gets messy. And it's about trusting yourself enough to be vulnerable. As you do the internal work, the external connection also thrives.

Our life journey is like following a treasure map where X marks the spot, only to realize you had the jewel in your pack all along. We forget we already have authentic love – we are pure love, it shines from our core. There is no quest required.

Young children, who are often closer to the source of One Love than adults, still seem to have this natural joy and a sense of wonder in them. They still have that 'new soul' smell – the fragrance of forever. As we grow up, it's so easy to become jaded, disillusioned, divided, defensive, tense, lost and lonely.

A lifetime of ego conditioning makes us seek out love, peace, contentment and surprise in all the wrong places. We try to look for 'the one' without realizing we are 'the one' we've been looking for. Every relationship shows you glimpses of this truth, if you look closely. A loving partner can help you remember you've been whole, you've been love, all along.

I hope that this book has given you greater clarity on love and relationships. I suspect that some of what I have shared is familiar to you already, because this isn't my knowledge alone, it belongs to all humanity, and anyone with an open, receptive heart will reach similar conclusions if they follow the path of truth and love. My intention was to illuminate the connection between the eternal love at life's centre and the way we reflect that with partners – and with everyone we encounter.

Now the journey is yours. May these words nurture growth as you shape your life with compassion and courage. The destination belongs to you as well – to realize you already are what you seek. Authentic love is your essence.

Keep this truth ever close: love is not just something to find but to be. Become it, express it, and your whole world transforms. Then through each thought, word and action, you will manifest this radiance living inside you. Your presence will enrich every life you touch.

Go shine your loving light, sweet friend.

Vex King.